Mull
and Iona
40 Favourite Walks

The authors and publisher have made every effort to ensure that the information in this publication is accurate, and accept no responsibility whatsoever for any loss, injury or inconvenience experienced by any person or persons whilst using this book.

published by
pocket mountains ltd
Holm Street, Moffat
Dumfries and Galloway
DG10 9EB

ISBN: 978-1-9070250-9-9

Printed in Poland

Introduction

Mull is the second largest island of the Inner Hebrides, its moorland peninsulas radiating out from a rugged heart of mountains and fringed by impressive coastal cliffs. The irregular shape of the island covers over 800 sq km with its convoluted coastline stretching for nearly 500km, but all this vast space is home to less than 3000 people. This gives a clue to the wild nature of the island, with a feeling of vastness and space that is greatly enhanced by the narrow, twisting island roads. It is perhaps no surprise that the island has become famed for its wildlife, with sea eagles soaring over all that magnificent terrain, roamed by red deer, and with otters, dolphins and seals frequently seen from the shore.

In spite of the tiny population when compared to the size of the island, Mull is well used to catering for visitors and the walks can often be combined with visits to attractions, craft studios, tea rooms or restaurants. Most walkers will also want to take advantage of one of the wildlife-spotting and scenic boat trips, including those to Staffa and Fingal's Cave, or out to Lunga and the Treshnish islands (packed with puffins in early summer). The sea eagle hide at Loch Frisa (pre-booking required) is a must for any amateur twitcher. Mull and Iona also have their share of excellent historical attractions, such as Iona Abbey and Duart Castle. A recent revival in the production of local and seasonal food means that many cafés and restaurants are now serving local seafood,

meat and cheese, not forgetting the local Oban Bay Brewery real ales and whisky from the Tobermory distillery, which does a great tour, perfect for a wet day.

How to use this guide

This book contains 40 varied walks located in all corners of the island and its two smaller neighbours, Iona and Ulva. Whilst many of the walks are on tracks and paths, Mull's high annual rainfall and peaty terrain mean that boggy ground is often encountered. Where this is particularly likely to be the case it is highlighted, but waterproof boots are recommended generally for any walking on Mull. The few mountain routes included in this book require full hillwalking gear and good navigation skills, but several of the coastal routes such as the walks to the Fossil Tree and to the Carsaig Arches are not to be underestimated. A sketch map accompanies each route; however, apart from a couple of the shortest waymarked trails, it is essential to carry and use an Ordnance Survey map.

There is no mountain rescue team on Mull, so even more than elsewhere it is crucial that anyone heading out for a walk is well prepared and has good navigation skills. On most of the walks, mobile phone reception is non-existent.

Access and dogs

Mull has a limited bus service which is geared towards the school day; however, with a bit of pre-planning and imagination it is possible to access many of the walks using a mix of public transport and taxis. Most of the routes are circular and the book indicates where public transport can be taken, although up to date timetables should be checked at the visitor information centres (Craignure and Tobermory) or with Traveline Scotland (travelinescotland.com).

Scotland has some of the most liberal access laws in Europe thanks to the Land Reform (Scotland) Act 2003. This gave walkers the right of access over most Scottish land away from residential buildings. With these rights come responsibilities as set out in the Scottish Outdoor Access Code which is worth familiarising yourself with. Mull is still a predominantly crofting landscape with sheep and cattle often grazing on open land; the land provides a rich habitat for many species of groundnesting birds. For these reasons dogs must be kept under close control during spring and early summer and at all times when livestock are present.

Wildlife

The Isle of Mull has become a byword for wildlife spotting. White-tailed or sea eagles were reintroduced on the nearby Isle of Rum from 1975 and became resident again on Mull. Recent TV programmes featuring the eagles, as well as the otters, deer and other wildlife on the island, have made it a top destination for both avid twitchers and more amateur wildlife enthusiasts. A number of companies have sprung up

offering wildlife safaris and tours as well as whale and bird watching boat trips.

The sea eagle is Britain's largest bird of prey and to see these massive creatures sweeping overhead is a memorable experience. The RSPB runs a viewing hide overlooking a nest site at Loch Frisa that is open to the public, although all visits must be booked in advance. This gives the chance to see the birds up close using scopes and binoculars and on CCTV; however, anyone undertaking many of the coastal and hill routes on the island is likely to be rewarded with a good sighting.

Otters on the other hand are more elusive, although those at Tobermory Harbour are getting canny to the regular food source from the fishing boats and are becoming less shy. On coastal walks look out for the tell-tale bright green grassy mounds made up from their nitrogren-rich spraint used to mark territories. Spotting otters requires much luck. However, seals are seen much more often, and boat trips provide opportunities to see the whales which frequent the waters in the spring and summer months.

One tiny creature amongst Mull's famed wildlife is less favoured by visitors – the midge. During the summer months these tiny biters come out in force on still, drizzly days, especially in the early morning and evening, though a slight wind or strong sunshine usually sees them off. A variety of repellents are available, many based on the chemical DEET and others containing bog-myrtle; many locals use Avon *Skin so Soft*.

History/Background

Arriving on Mull many visitors' first impression is how green the island is, closely followed by just how tortuous, windy and bumpy many of the roads are. The verdant green of much of the island is a result of relatively heavy rainfall combined with the warming effects of the Gulf Stream; there are also broad forestry plantations which have clothed large areas of the island in conifers.

Although much of the land on Mull is still crofted, many areas have been given over to common grazings rather than the more intensive crofting practices of the past. The scattered settlements, empty glens, and numerous ruined crofts and summer sheilings are testament to a time when Mull was heavily populated. Human settlement here goes back a long way, evidenced by the forts and crannogs built by residents in the Iron Age.

At its peak in the 18th and 19th centuries the island's population stood at around 10,000. Most people were tenants of a few large landowners; as well as a number of trades and fishing, many crofters were employed gathering and processing seaweed for a number of uses. The collapse of the kelp industry, combined with the potato famine, propelled many landowners into clearing the land of their tenants to make way for more profitable sheep. Some of the clearances were particularly brutal with reports of tenants being burnt out of their homes.

A poorhouse was established in Tobermory and many families emigrated – hence the establishment of Calgary and Iona in Canada.

Mull also became popular as a destination on the Grand Tour with Fingal's Cave on Staffa a particular draw, together with Mackinnon's Cave and the Fossil Tree.

Planning your visit

Although visitor numbers are lost amongst Mull's vast empty acres, the island's popularity means that during the summer months both the car ferries and accommodation on the island can be booked up well in advance. This is especially true on Saturday ferry sailings from Oban. If travelling from Fort William or the north, the 15-minute crossing from Lochaline is worth checking out – this cannot be pre-booked. Ferry prices and availability can be checked online with Calmac (calmac.co.uk).

Mull has a good range of places to stay. A number of luxury serviced and self-catering properties have recently sprung up as well as hostels, campsites (including the static canvas sheilings available for rent at Craignure) and many good B&Bs. At Calgary Bay locals have responded to demand – and helped mitigate damage to the fragile machair – by setting up a wild camping area; similarly the community at Dervaig added bunkrooms when the local hall was being refurbished.

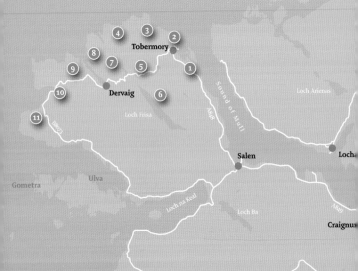

The array of multi-coloured houses fringing the fine natural harbour at Tobermory make up one of Mull's most familiar picture-postcard scenes. The town, famed to a generation of children as television's 'Balamory', is by far the largest settlement on the island and despite its location in the far north it remains the main hub for services.

Tobermory has a good mixture of shops and craft studios and is home to the distillery which always provides a warming glow on a cold day. In better weather boat trips depart from the harbour to seek out whales, dolphins and other sea mammals. Aros Park is a good place to explore with

children, with a good play park and barbecue area. Compared to other parts of the island, the landscape here is gentler, with the attractive coastline fringed by forestry and rolling moors inland.

West from Tobermory is Dervaig, a village whose picturesque main street was the result of being built to a plan by the Laird of Coll in 1799. At the head of an inlet which penetrates far inland, it feels far from the open sea – a reminder of the convoluted nature of the coastline. Further west once more is Calgary, a tiny settlement set above one of Mull's finest and best known beaches.

6

North Mull and Tobermory

Aros Park and Tobermory

Distance 5.5km **Time** 2 hours
Terrain paths, steep in places and
sometimes muddy **Map** OS Explorer 374
Access bus to Tobermory; ferry from
Kilchoan on Ardnamurchan peninsula
to Tobermory in summer

**Enjoy fabulous views of Tobermory on
this varied coastal and woodland wander,
taking in a tumbling waterfall and a
lochan bursting with water lilies.**

Start from the Ledaig car park which sits
at the south end of Tobermory's harbour
front, just beyond the distillery. From here
you get the classic view of the brightly
painted houses, immortalised for a certain
generation as the home of television's
'Balamory'. Miss Hoolie and Josie Jump
aside, there is a visitor centre and toilets in

the modern Taigh Solais building
overlooking the sea at the far end of the
car park. Start from here, looking out
for the path signed for Aros Park that
starts between this building and a
restaurant. The path climbs steeply giving
changing perspectives of the harbour
and houses.

Pass the Sput Dubh waterfall and at the
barrier take the signed path to the right to
head up steps, rewarded with glimpses of the
Ardnamurchan peninsula between the
Scots pines. Branch left at a fork, heading
down more steps to a picnic table with a
great view across the water. Keep on the
main path, ignoring steps up to the right,
to cross a bridge by a pool. Turn sharp
right at a bench to climb again, this time
on steep zigzags.

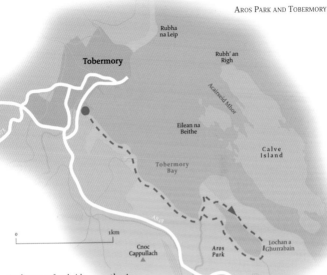

At the top a footbridge over the Aros burn gives a good view of the waterfall as the water rushes down on its short journey to the sea. A path on the right allows a closer inspection of the falls. The walk, however, continues ahead until a signed junction where you keep straight on, following the sign for The Pier. After another bridge turn right at the T-junction next to the barn.

A short detour to the left can be made to visit the pier, otherwise continue until the route splits into three. Take the left-hand path and then immediately turn right to start heading round Lochan a'Ghurrabain, keeping the water on your right. In summer the water is a mass of flowering waterlilies; younger walkers may be more interested in the children's play area on the left.

The lochan is an artificial feature created when the surrounding land was landscaped to provide parkland to Aros House. The house was built in 1825 and overlooked the loch, but was demolished in the 1960s. The numerous rhododendrons – which the Forestry Commission has been battling to control – provide a beautiful mass of colourful flowers in spring.

Bear right at the junction at the head of the loch, keeping to the lochside route after a footbridge and then climbing to the Aros car park and picnic area. Cross to the far side to pick up the path past the toilets. The path soon reaches a fork, take the right-hand branch to rejoin the outward path then turn left along this to retrace your steps to Tobermory.

◀ Tobermory Harbour

Rubha nan Gall Lighthouse

Distance 5.5km **Time** 2 hours
Terrain very muddy year round – wellies
recommended! **Map** OS Explorer 374
Access bus to Tobermory; ferry from
Kilchoan on Ardnamurchan peninsula
to Tobermory in summer

This is a great walk from the centre of
Tobermory to the atmospheric lighthouse
at Rubha nan Gall – a fine spot to watch
wildlife or just relax overlooking the water
to the mainland. An optional return route
offers a steep climb to the golf course and
an excellent view over Tobermory.

If driving, the best place to park is the
Ledaig car park, just on the right as you
come down the hill into Tobermory. From
here start by following the main street
around the seafront, passing the brightly
coloured properties that give Tobermory
its trademark appearance. Once past the

RNLI shop but before the Calmac pier head
up the path which slopes uphill through
the trees on the left.

Ignore the steps up on the left at the old
cannon emplacement – these steps are
used on the way back if the higher return is
taken. The cannon which once stood here
is long gone, thought to have been melted
down for the war effort during the Second
World War. Stay on the narrow path,
keeping an eye out for a steep path sloping
down on the right. This short detour leads
to a small beach which was popular during
Victorian times, when bathing boxes
wheeled ladies discreetly into the water to
take their healthy dip away from prying
eyes. The remains of the old bathing pool
can still be made out.

Continue on the path,
which is very muddy in
places, with glimpses of the

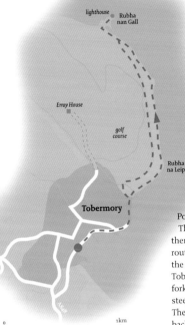

lighthouse Rubha
nan Gall

Erray House

golf
course

Rubha
na Leip

Tobermory

0   1km

The lighthouse itself was built by the Stevenson clan which had a virtual monopoly on the construction of Scottish lighthouses. This particular one was built by Robert, the grandfather of author Robert Louis Stevenson, in 1857; the keepers lived in the nearby cottages until the light was fully automated in 1960. The name Rubha nan Gall means 'Stranger's Point' in Gaelic.

The easiest return is the same way, but there is an alternative longer and rougher route which climbs up and then runs along the edge of the golf course overlooking Tobermory. For this route take the right fork just before the memorial to climb steeply on a sometimes overgrown path. There are great views of the lighthouse back over your shoulder as you climb. The path skirts along the top of the cliff, passing through dense undergrowth. Keep straight ahead at a metal post and cross a stile onto the golf course. Turn left, keeping to the very edge of the course and taking care not to disturb play – follow the green and white posts. Watch out for stray shots as you pass the back of the 5th hole and soon the path reaches a metal gate. When the path splits bear left, continuing left onto a road and turning left down the steps immediately after the war memorial. These return you to the outward path where a right turn leads back to the start.

sea on the right through the trees. Keep right at a fork to stay on the level as the views begin to open out. Soon the lighthouse can be seen ahead. A few steps off the path to the right is a memorial where a view indicator helps to identify the mainland peaks, settlements and islands. The main path passes in front of the first lighthouse cottage to reach the lighthouse causeway. Keep a sharp eye out for otters – easier to see in the water, they are quickly lost amongst the seaweed and rocks once they come ashore.

Ardmore shore

Distance **7.25km** Time **2 hours**
Terrain **forestry track and rougher path**
Map **OS Explorer 374** Access **nearest bus
stop is in Tobermory, 6km from start**

**Easy going forestry tracks lead down to
the shoreline at Ardmore Bay where a
wildlife hide offers a good spot to watch
for passing otters, birds and seals.**

This walk starts from the Ardmore
Forestry Commission car park which is
signed from the Glengorm road – itself
just off the Dervaig Road from Tobermory.
The parking area is a short way down the
track. From here continue along the track
with the occasional view of the sea ahead.
At the junction, go left – the right-hand
route is used for the return. At the next
turn take the signed path on the right to
pass the ruins of Penalbanach, which was
farmed until the 1930s. Recent felling by

the Forestry Commission has allowed the
ruins to emerge from their blanket of Sitka
Spruce; when re-planted there will be more
broadleaved species to soften the edges of
the plantation and improve biodiversity.

The path continues downhill towards
Ardmore Bay. Just before the shore is
reached a detour to the left leads to a hide.
Overlooking a sheltered bay, this is a great
place to watch birds and seals and possibly
an otter or two; or just for shelter if the
weather is inclement. Look out for the
small humps of bright green grass where
the luxuriant growth is fertilised by otter
spraint, rich in fish bones and thought to
be a way of marking territory. Otters appear
to follow the same Murphy's law rule of
wildlife watching applicable to many
elusive creatures – you will see them by
chance on the days when you forget to
bring your binoculars or camera. Patience

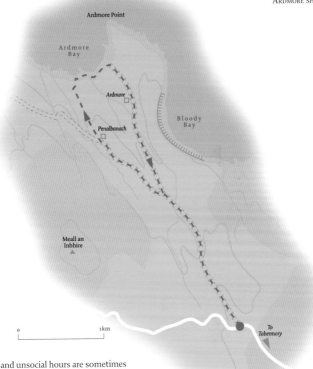

Ardmore Point

Ardmore Bay

Ardmore

Penalbanach

Bloody Bay

Meall an
Inbhire

0   1km

To
Tobermory

and unsocial hours are sometimes
rewarded, though, and a glimpse of one
of these beautiful creatures is a highlight
of any walk.

Follow the shore path. Wooden steps
lead to a picnic table boasting great views
across the water to the Ardnamurchan
Peninsula, the most westerly point of
mainland Britain. The islands of Skye, Rum
and Muck can be seen on a clear day and,
further west, the flatter Coll and Tiree.

Another rough section of shore path

leads on to the edge of the plantation from
where the path heads inland again. Once
out of the impenetrable gloom of the
dense trees the ruins of Ardmore village
are passed on the left. Cross the burn and
climb the gentle path until it meets a
forestry track. Go straight ahead, soon
reaching the junction with the outward
track; turn left to retrace the route uphill
to the start.

◀ Rocky shore at Ardmore Bay

Dun Ara and Glengorm Castle

Distance 3.75km **Time** 1 hour 30
Terrain grassy track, boggy in places,
steep and rocky short climb to Dun Ara
Map OS Explorer 374 **Access** no public
transport to start

Set out from the baronial splendour of
Glengorm Castle, crossing grazing land to
reach the site of Dun Ara fort standing
guard above the sea. This wild stretch of
coastline has plenty of wildlife-watching
opportunities as well as offering the
chance to take a dip yourself in the
seawater bathing pool.

Glengorm Castle, completed in 1860,
boasts all the features typical of the Scots
Baronial style so popular in Victorian
times: turrets, towers, gothic arches,
imposing stonework and grand entrances.
It is signed off the B8073 just west of
Tobermory. Follow the minor road, head
through the white gates and then fork
right for the car park near the steading
which accommodates a coffee shop and

gallery. Start from the patio outside the
coffee shop, and after crossing the bridge
take the track to the right (SP Dun Ara and
the Bathing Pool). Head through the gate
and continue on the track to cross pastures
as you head towards the coast.

The Glengorm estate is very extensive,
and the castle can be seen up to the left.
The castle itself was built by James Forsyth,
notorious locally for his part in the
Highland Clearances that saw Mull's
population fall dramatically. Local folklore
has it that Forsyth was duped into naming
the castle and estate Glengorm after
asking for advice from a local gaelic
speaker who suggested the name because
of the blue/grey smoke that hung in the
glen after the burning of the tenants'
homes, 'gorm' meaning blue. Forsyth
himself did not live to see the castle
completed as he perished in a riding
accident. Since Victorian times the castle
has passed through a number of different
hands, starting out as a sporting estate

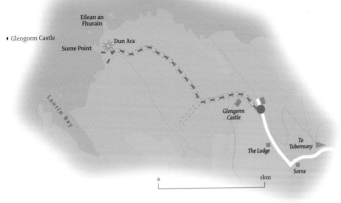

Eilean an
Fhurain

◄ Glengorm Castle

Some Point   ☼ Dun Ara

Laorin Bay

Glengorm
Castle

The Lodge   To
                          Tobermory

Some

0   1km

lodge and now being run as holiday
accommodation with fresh produce for the
island grown in the walled garden.

As the route nears the coast,
Ardnamurchan Point can be seen across
the water, although the tall lighthouse at
the Point remains hidden from view. Just
after a second gate fork right onto a grassy
track. When a T-junction is reached an
impressive group of three tall standing
stones can be seen over to the left.
Otherwise turn right towards a gate,
climbing a stile to cross a field and keeping
the stone wall on your right. Once down
the slope head over a stile next to another
gate and follow the faint and curving track
through two further gates. The track curves
right to head behind two rocky outcrops
after a third gate. The third, and more
distinctive, hummock is the site of the
ancient fort of Dun Ara that sits atop the
natural stone ramparts.

Cliffs surround most of Dun Ara so
follow the path to the right which leads to

a natural break in the rocks where a path
climbs steeply to the summit. The remains
of the curtain stone and lime wall which
fortified the perimeter can still be seen.
It is thought that the site was originally an
iron-age fort on which a later castle was
built and occupied at least from the 1600s
if not earlier, probably as a stronghold of
the MacKinnons who held extensive lands
on Mull from the mid 1300s onwards.
Surrounding Dun Ara are the remains of a
farming settlement and it is thought the
ancient harbour nearby would have been
the main approach to the castle.

The strategic importance of the site can
be appreciated on a swift glance over the
sea with good views to Ardnamurchan,
Coll and Tiree. Once down off Dun Ara
continue along the track to reach the coast
where the brave can be tempted into a spot
of wild swimming in the remains of a
sheltered bathing pool. For the less hardy
it's still a great spot to sit back and watch
for seals and otters, or eagles overhead.

15

Crater Loch

Distance **3km** Time **1 hour 30**
Terrain **rough and boggy moorland**
Map **OS Explorer 374** Access **no public
transport to start**

**Climb up to make a circuit around the rim
of the Crater Loch – Lochan 's Airde Beinn.
This short but rugged and boggy walk
feels like a proper adventure with
stunning views, though your imagination
will have to provide the molten lava and
steaming sulphur.**

The approach to Crater Lake is from the
B8073 Tobermory to Dervaig road. There is
no proper parking area, just a small lay-by
situated immediately before a ruined
house if approaching from Tobermory,

opposite Loch Meadhoin and just beyond
the edge of the forestry. If there is no room
here there is an old quarry approximately
half a kilometre back along the road
towards Tobermory which can be used.

To start the ascent, climb the makeshift
stile from the lay-by and bear slightly left.
Leaving the ruined cottage behind, the
route, which can be indistinct at first when
the bracken is high, keeps the forestry edge
well to the right (east). As you climb the
peak ahead becomes more prominent and
it is possible to imagine the molten lava
and energy emerging from the stack 60
million years ago. As well as the caldera
remains here, there are volcanic basalt
columns at numerous points on the

Mull coast including Carsaig and Ardtun as well as the famous Fingal's Cave on neighbouring Staffa. The island's highest peak, Ben More, is also an extinct volcano.

At a fork keep straight ahead, the right-hand path being the return route. This area is often very wet underfoot. Mull has some of the UK's heaviest annual rainfall at 4500mm – with rain falling on average at some point during 283 days of the year. However, in common with much of the west coast the Atlantic breezes keep the weather systems moving – the weather is so changeable that the islanders say you can experience all four seasons in one day.

A short, steep climb leads to a cairn on the edge above the loch. From here bear left to walk around the rim of the crater, sticking to the high ground above the loch to enjoy great views in all directions. Once you reach a dip before the final climb which would complete the circuit, cross the outflow of the loch and instead take the small path which descends by the burn. This rocky and narrow path stays on the right-hand side of the stone wall before eventually bending to the right to rejoin the outward route and return to the start.

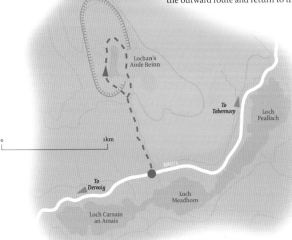

Lochan's Airde Beinn

To Tobermory

Loch Peallach

0   1km

To Dervaig

B8073

Loch Meadhon

Loch Carnain an Amais

◀ Lochan 's Airde Beinn

Speinne Mor

Distance 9km Time 3 hours
Terrain rough and boggy path over
moorland Map OS Explorer 374
Access no public transport to start

This boggy but satisfying climb over the moors to reach the highest point in north Mull is rewarded by panoramic views.

A tiny disused quarry provides parking space for three or four cars at the start of this walk. Find it by heading past the western end of the last of the Mishnish Lochs, Loch Carnain an Amais, on the Tobermory to Dervaig road (B8073). The parking space is at the top of the winding descent to

Loch Frisa and is a great viewpoint. From here follow a clear path through bracken to a gate and then go up through some small crags, always keeping to the highest ground.

The faint and sometimes boggy path heads up the broad nose of Speinne Mor. A quick look back is rewarded by the three Mishnish Lochs strung out in a sparkling line below. Long Loch Frisa eventually comes into view on the right. From here the route stays slightly to the right (SW)

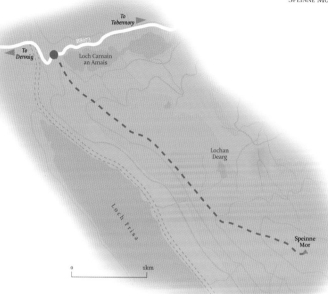

side of the ridge line and crosses several areas of bare rock which provide welcome relief from the generally wet ground underfoot. Soon Mull's highest peak, Ben More, comes into view in the distance. The route picks up and follows a line of old rusting fenceposts, a great navigational aid in poor conditions. Dip to cross a burn flowing from Lochan Dearg to the left before tackling the final climb.

Keep following the fenceposts to pass a lonely and redundant gate and head over steeper ground. As the gradient eases the fenceposts leave the ridge and traverse the side of Speinne Mor. Leave them here and head east, bearing left to reach the main ridge. The crest is not well defined; keep heading for the highest ground and at the last moment the trig point, surrounded by a large rocky shelter, comes into view. On the final approach there are great views down to Tobermory on the left. The summit itself is a wonderful viewpoint, especially looking inland to the peaks of Ardnamurchan and Morvern across the Sound of Mull. It is possible to make a circuit by descending to the track alongside Loch Frisa at Lettermore, but this is not recommended as the way down is very steep and hard to locate. Instead it is better to retrace the outward route, hopefully rewarded with views of Coll, Tiree and the distant Outer Hebrides ahead.

◀ Tobermory and the mainland from Speinne Mor summit

Loch an Torr and Glengorm

Distance 10.25km **Time** 3 hours
Terrain clear forestry and moorland tracks
Map OS Explorer 374 **Access** no public
transport to start

This walk on a shared-use path from picturesque Loch an Torr makes a wide circuit of forests and moorland.

Start from the Loch Torr Forestry Commission car park which is marked by a large sign on the right of the B8073 Tobermory to Dervaig road, soon after a long winding descent. Head along the track and keep an eye out for cyclists as this route is also popular with mountain bikers, including those from the local club who use it for training and time trials. Go through a gate and keep straight on at a

fork to climb uphill in a series of zigzags. There are good views down to the loch which is a favourite haunt of fly fishermen trying their luck for brown trout and the occasional salmon.

Part of the forest has been felled, allowing views beyond the rolling hills to the spiky towers of the Rum Cuillin in the far distance. After 4km turn sharp right at a junction signed for the bike route to Loch Frisa. This soon leads to a wide but rickety wooden bridge over the Mingarry Burn. Pass through a felled area – going across the end of another track to finally leave the forestry plantations behind at a gate. Continue up open moorland to reach another track at a T-junction. Turn right here – again signed as the bike route for

Loch Frisa north (the left branch eventually goes to Ardmore).

As in many areas of Scotland, mountain biking is really taking off on Mull with a number of purpose-built trails and skills areas being developed, but the island also remains popular with cycle tourers who can use the ferries at either end to make a stunning tour. The bike trail at Loch Torr hosts an annual bike race but with mud and riders flying in all directions you are likely to get a fair bit of notice if you do clash with that day. Many of the forest tracks on Mull make excellent off-road route but the ones at Loch Frisa are

particularly good as you can hope to catch sight of sea eagles and the route is generally too long in the forest to make for pleasant walking.

The track passes through two gates; continue straight ahead when another track branches right. Eventually a fork is reached where the track meets the remains of the old road. Keep ahead, following the cycle sign through a gate to reach the modern road. Turn right to follow the tarmac for the walk back to the start by Loch an Torr.

◄ Glengorm forest trail

21

Quinish Point

Distance 12.75km **Time** 4 hours
Terrain track and grassy fields
Map OS Explorer 374 **Access** bus (494) to
Dervaig (except Sundays)

**Head out onto the Quinish peninsula from
Dervaig, passing a magnificent standing
stone, through woods and grazings to
reach the headland. From this secluded
spot the fabulous seascape takes in the
islands of Coll, Rum, Skye and even the
Outer Hebrides on a clear day.**

Dervaig is a picturesque small village
with a shop and inn – note the round tower
of the white church near the shore. The
walk starts along the road to Cuin, but
there is no parking along the road so if
driving it is best to leave your car in Dervaig
and begin from the village. Head up the
main street of houses, passing the shop
and bearing left at the end. Pass the public

toilets and the last houses before the
singletrack road leads on – with lovely loch
views – to the houses at Cuin, where you
may catch sight of a member of the local
seal colony. At the end of the public road
continue ahead on the track, soon crossing
a cattle grid. Head through the Quinish
gateposts into the woods, ignoring the
track leading to the house on the right.

The mixed woodland is alive with birds
in spring and summer and provides a very
pleasant couple of kilometres. At a
junction take the main track which bends
right to reach Home Farm. At the fork
immediately beyond keep straight on,
ignoring the larger track to the right, and
go straight on again at the next junction
where a left-hand fork leads to Quinish
House. Follow the track through a couple
of gates and out onto open grazings with
sea views. Stay on the main track which

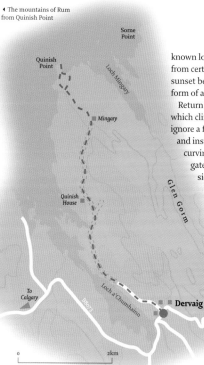

◀ The mountains of Rum from Quinish Point

known locally as Calliach, old woman, and from certain angles, particularly with the sunset behind, the stone does take on the form of a cloaked woman.

Return to the route and follow the track which climbs to the right. Further on ignore a faint track heading through a gate and instead stay on the main track curving right, soon passing through a gate and then turning left on the far side of the wall. Mingary can now be seen ahead. Go through a gate before the house, then leave the main track to bear left on a faint grassy track signed Quinish Point. Pass below crags and head through another gate before descending, with views over the hillock of Dun Ban to the isle of Coll beyond. The track then swings right to reach a second hillock, Dun Dubh, on the point itself. From here you should be rewarded with a stunning view with the jagged peaks of both the Rum and Skye Cuillin visible as well as the mountains of North Uist. The return is by the same route, or if you don't mind wet feet you can follow the shore back as far as Dun Ban before cutting up left to rejoin the outward track.

climbs gradually; at the next fork our route follows the uphill branch to the right, but a short detour ahead leads to a prominent standing stone. Of the four remaining stones here only one now stands upright, almost 3m high. Archaeologists believe that there were originally five standing stones all aligned towards the major southern moonrise. The upright stone is

Langamull Beach

Distance **6.25km** Time **2 hours**
Terrain **good track and waymarked paths**
Map **OS Explorer 374** Access **no public transport to the start**

Langamull beach (Chrossapol Bay on maps) is a beguiling mix of dazzling white sand and blue water backed by the dramatic mountains of Rum and Skye. Even in bad weather this is a great place to explore; on a hot summer day you might only have to share the sunbathing spots with the resident sheep.

The North West Mull Community Company – a local charity – manages two woodlands including Langamull with the aim of creating jobs and funding for affordable housing and other projects. The car park is on the north side of the B8073, midway between Dervaig and Calgary

and is marked by a colourful sign. From here walk down the wide forestry track, bearing left at a fork to stay on the older track. A gate leads out of the trees; keep on the track as it follows the edge of the plantation.

Cattle and sheep graze here so dogs need to be kept under tight control at all times – extra care is needed when the livestock have young. Soon the sea can be glimpsed ahead, with the islands of Mull, Eigg and Skye visible on a clear day. Ignore the sign to Kildavie Settlement (which is instead visited on the return), and head through the gate ahead, passing to the left of the stone steading and bearing left on a grassy path. Go through the gate ahead, ignoring the gate nearer to the sea, and head directly across a field with a stone wall on your right to reach another gate leading

◀ White sands of Langamull Bay

onto open ground. The track splits here; the left branch makes a pleasant detour to Port Langamull but we turn right with an eye on the gleaming white sands ahead.

Another gate leads to the final stretch – bear right onto a smaller path heading directly for the beach, with sheep lazily scattered around. The beach, with its rocky headlands, crystal-clear waters and springy green turf, makes a perfect spot for a bit of nature watching, relaxing or letting little feet run wild.

On the return it is possible to delve into the woods to uncover the remains of the old settlement of Kildavie. Return along the track to the signed path for Kildavie; heading through a high deer gate. Very soon the path, marked by red arrows, plunges into the thick spruce trees before bearing right. Watch out for tree roots as the way turns right at a T-junction to head down to a bridge. Cross this, and halfway along the next straight section keep any eye out for a marked turn on the right which leads up to a clearing containing the turf and stone remains of Kildavie. This was once a sizeable

settlement and the remains of a corn drying kiln and a number of houses have been uncovered by archaeologists. Nature is slowly winning a battle here as foxgloves and nettles colonise the once-human haunts. Return to the car park by retracing your steps to the main track.

Art and nature at Calgary Bay

Distance 3km Time 1 hour 30
Terrain woodland path, narrow track
along shore, muddy in places with some
wooden steps which can be slippery
Map OS Explorer 374 Access bus (494)
from Tobermory (except Sun)

At Calgary Bay the Atlantic has sculpted a beautiful arc of white sand to make one of Mull's finest beaches. This walk follows a trail of artwork to reach the beach. Children and adults alike will love this route, with a good tearoom to finish.

If approaching from Dervaig, the large yellow-hued Calgary Farmhouse on the right-hand side of the road as you drive down the hill makes a good landmark. The car park for the Art in Nature Sculpture Trail is directly opposite. Start by crossing the road and passing the tearoom, or stopping in first if the cakes look too tempting. Bear right after the tearoom to visit the gallery; the walk starts from the far side. If the gallery is closed turn left to pass alongside; either way, the mill pond is soon reached. An aluminium sculpture called *Peace Cascade* hangs above the water.

The sculpture trail was established in Calgary Farm Wood in 1999, responding to trees that themselves have been sculpted by the westerly winds. Some of the art works have been created by the local community and others by resident

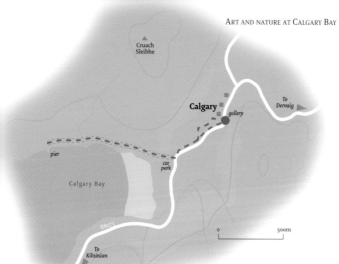

sculptor Matthew Reade, supplemented by commissions from other artists. After passing the *Calgary Mosaic*, ignore the steps and continue following the stream downhill. An old sawmill is passed on the left, followed by the *Flotsam and Jetsam* log.

Follow the path as it weaves through some majestic mature trees. Keep an eye out for a living willow tunnel, the Iona pebble mosaic and the *Leaf Seat* on the right. Ignore any paths off to the right and eventually a kissing gate at the edge of the wood is reached. Pass through, past the sheep and boat to reach the road beyond.

Follow the road to the right, almost immediately turning right again to the car park for Calgary Bay. Keep on the track which leaves from the right of the car park, passing through a kissing gate beside a farm gate. The track heads round the north

side of the bay, giving stunning views back over the white sand. The rocky lump on the right is the site of an ancient fort. At the end of the track an old harbour and pier is reached – a lovely place for a break and a spot of wildlife watching.

Before returning to complete the second half of the sculpture walk you may want to explore the sands which look tropical even under threatening skies. Head back along the track and road to the gate to the sculpture walk; pass through and take the first turn on the left. *In Dreaming* combines a copper figure on a steel bed under the trees. A little way further up the hill is a wonderful vantage point over the bay. The main path will lead you back through the trees to the wooden steps above the mill pond, but detours along meandering side paths reveal more sculptures hidden amongst the twisted trees.

Treshnish coast and the Whisky Cave

Distance 11km **Time** 4 hours
Terrain track, rough coast and moorland, very boggy in places; dogs must be kept under tight control **Map** OS Explorer 374
Access nearest bus stop is at Calgary Bay, 3km from start

Often billed as the finest coastal walk on Mull, this circular around the Treshnish peninsula takes in dramatic cliffs, varied wildlife and fascinating historical remains. It includes a visit to a legendary whisky cave where the best 'moonshine' on Mull was once distilled.

The walk crosses unfenced working croft land and open moorland where dogs have caused problems in the past. The landowners are happy for people to walk this spectacular route but ask that if dogs have to be taken they are kept under tight control to prevent disturbance to sheep and groundnesting birds.

The walk starts from the B8073 between Calgary and Burg. There is limited parking in an unmarked old quarry a short distance south of the track signed for Treshnish and Haunn cottages, just beyond Ensay. Head back along the road and follow the track through sparse woodland before passing the old schoolhouse. After a cattle grid there are good views north across the water to the Mornish peninsula. Soon the cottages at Treshnish are reached; turn left onto the track in front of the white building to pass above the cottages and through a gate. Keep on the track, passing through another gate and bearing right to pass a sheep fank and shed. Continue across the moor and through a further gate to approach the remote cottages at Haunn.

Turn right onto a signed path just before the cottages. This leads through two more gates before bearing left down towards the sea across a steep slope. The remains of an iron-age fort sits on top of the prominent rocky cliff on the right. Here the path ends; keep following the coastline staying close to the clifftops above the grassy raised beach.

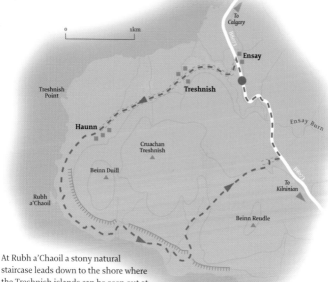

At Rubh a'Chaoil a stony natural staircase leads down to the shore where the Treshnish islands can be seen out at sea. Home to a large puffin colony, a boat trip to the islands is often rewarded with sightings of marine mammals as well as numerous seabirds. At this point you can either stay below the cliffs following a sheep track above the boulders or take the easier route which climbs back up to the left and continues along the clifftop; the two options rejoin in about half a kilometre.

Cross a steep slope before passing two inlets. At the third inlet, identifiable by its steep ivy-clad sides, it is possible to descend the grassy gully with care to reach a pebble beach from which the Whisky Cave can be explored on the right. Here illicit whisky was distilled far from the prying eyes of the excise men – the remains of the stone still are still clearly visible.

Back on the coast path cross a burn and after 300m follow the remains of an old dyke and then a faint path which zigzags up the slope passing a waterfall. Soon the atmospheric remains of the village of Crackaig are reached. Crackaig was abandoned after a devastating typhoid outbreak. The path bears right to re-cross the burn, reaching the remains of another settlement, Glac Gugairidh. Continue climbing over the moor, following marker posts and aiming for the right of a white house, to reach a track. Once at the road turn left to return to the start.

◀ Heading along the Treshnish clifftop

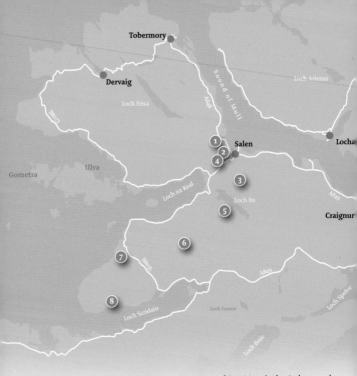

Mull narrows to a slender waist at its midpoint, where the east and west coasts are just 4km apart. Here is the village of Salen, a focal point for road transport on Mull, making it one of the best bases for touring the island. The setting here is gentle with an attractive shoreline, but heading south and west the landscape becomes increasingly wild and dramatic, ultimately rising to the great peak of Ben More, Britain's highest island summit outwith Skye.

Beyond Ben More is the Ardmeanach Peninsula, as rugged a tract of country as you will find anywhere. A remarkable road passes beneath the high cliffs of Gribun before cutting inland to Loch Scridain, but the peninsula itself is roadless; a wilderness of crags, heather and scree populated by mountain goats. Two walks lead out into this area – a short but rugged excursion to a great sea cave in the north, and the longer, awe-inspiring route past the Burg in the south.

Tomsleibhe Bothy, Glen Forsa ▶

Salen, Central Mull and Ardmeanach

Glen Aros

Distance 1.5km **Time** 30 minutes
Terrain waymarked forestry track
Map OS Explorer 374 **Access** nearest bus
stop is in Salen, 3km from start

**This short but pleasant forestry circuit
near Loch Frisa visits the site of an old
chapel and graveyard with views towards
Ben More.**

Lying in the remote centre of north
Mull, Loch Frisa is famous for its nesting
sea eagles. With a bit of luck you may well
see the giant birds, once described as flying
barn doors due to their massive wing span,
overhead on this short walk which delves
into Salen Wood, a forestry plantation
just to the east of the loch. For an almost
guaranteed sighting during the nesting
season, however, book yourself onto one
of the hide visits at 10am and 1pm,
Monday to Friday. Walkers and cyclists can
access the hide from the track at the start
of this walk but it is only open for the pre-
booked tours.

Just north of Salen, turn off the A848
Tobermory road and take the Forestry
Commission track past the offices to reach
a car park and picnic area a short distance

further on. This route is waymarked with red marker posts.

Start by continuing along the track on foot, passing through a gate into the dark, densely-planted forestry. After a bench, keep an eye out for a Forest Walk sign indicating a path which leads off uphill to the right. Take this path, climbing through the trees until the old burial ground of Cill an Alein is seen on the left. It is worth heading into the burial ground to examine the old graves and ruins; this is an atmospheric spot with a view to the summit of Ben More if the weather is kind.

Return to the main path and continue uphill until a junction with a forestry track is reached. Turn right here, follow the track and eventually pass through a gate. On the final descent back towards the car park there are more open views ahead; as well as the sea eagles for which this part of Mull is famed, keep an eye out for hen harriers, buzzards and golden eagles, all resident in the area.

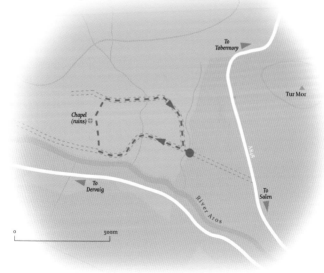

To
Tobermory

Tur Mòr

Chapel
(ruins)

A849

To
Dervaig

To
Salen

River Aros

0   500m

◀ Cill an Alein burial ground

33

Cnoc na Sroine

Distance 6.25km **Time** 2 hours 30
Terrain track, rough hill paths, boggy in
places **Map** OS Explorer 374 **Access** bus to
Salen from Craignure and Tobermory

**This varied circuit from Salen starts along
the coastline before crossing fields to
reach Glenaros House. It climbs up onto
the moors to visit an iron-age fort with
superb all-round views before making a
boggy descent to return via the woods
above the village.**

Salen has been settled since ancient
times and today boasts a pub, restaurant,
shop and post office amid a small cluster
of houses. There is parking near the
public toilets on the northern side of the
village off the road to Tobermory. From
here the walk begins by heading north
along the road verge, taking care as this
section of single-track road can be busy
if you coincide with the rush to or from
the ferries.

Look out for otters in the bay, decorated
with the hulks of wrecked fishing boats.
After passing a jetty keep an eye out
for a gate on the far side of the road
(SP Footpath to Glenaros Farm). Go
through the gate and up a grassy lane
through lovely woodland with views over
the Sound of Mull and the ruins of Aros
Castle to the north. This was built in the
13th century and served as headquarters
for the Clan MacDougall, Clan Donald
and Clan Maclean.

Go through a series of three farm gates
before Glenaros House comes into view
ahead. As the house draws closer head
through two further gates to pass well to
the left of the main house, reaching a
surfaced track by the old white
farmworkers' cottage. Cross the track and
head through the gate opposite, bearing
left across the often muddy field. Soon a
rough track emerges; follow this, climbing
gently with a stone wall on your left until

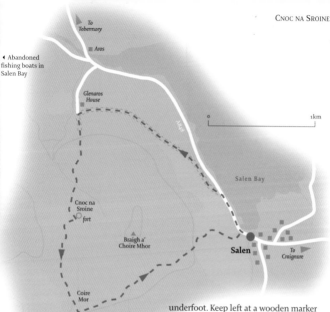

◀ Abandoned
fishing boats in
Salen Bay

To
Tobermory

Aros

Glenaros
House

Aros

0   1km

Salen Bay

Cnoc na
Sroine
fort

Braigh a'
Choire Mhor

Salen

To
Craignure

Coire
Mor

more open moorland is reached. Ford a small burn and head towards the grassy mound topped by a cairn. This is Cnoc na Sroine, once the site of an iron age fort – some of the original stones of the thick outer walls can still be seen. The best way up to the top is to continue on the path, climbing to the right of the knoll before turning left to detour up to the summit. This is a wonderful viewpoint for the Morvern peninsula on the mainland as well as Mull's eastern coastline.

Return to the main path and continue as it climbs to the highest point. Beyond this the descent is gradual but muddy

underfoot. Keep left at a wooden marker post to follow a clear path slightly left of the sparse birchwood. Eventually this leads to another path traversing the hillside. Turn left and climb through the fragments of woodland at Doire nam Pioghaid; in places it may be necessary to use sheep tracks on either side to avoid the boggiest sections. The path improves and heads across open ground with good views of Salen ahead. It leads into the wood at Airigh Mhic Dhom nuill, a mix of large oaks, birches and other native species. This provides a lovely end to the walk as the path descends steeply through the trees to reach Salen next to the old church. A right turn and a short section of road will bring you back to the start.

Beinn Talaidh

Distance 18km **Time** 5 hours 30
Terrain good track, then pathless
moorland and very steep grassy ascent,
stony ground higher up; hillwalking gear
and navigation skills needed
Map OS Explorer 375 **Access** nearest bus
stop is in Salen, 2.25km from start

Beinn Talaidh is one of Mull's most
prominent mountains, rising at the very
heart of the island, and as such is a great
viewpoint. The approach walk along Glen
Forsa is more enjoyable than the shorter
but more brutal ascent from the south;
this route passes a bothy at the foot of the
mountain which makes a good turning
point if a shorter lower-level walk is
preferred. Glen Forsa is grazed by cattle;
give them a wide berth, special care is
needed by walkers with dogs.

The entrance to Glen Forsa is found off
the A849 between Craignure and Salen at a
short section of road which strangely splits
into separate carriageways; the track is
signed 'Glen Forsa Estate only'. A short way
along the track is a parking area; from this
point access up the glen is restricted to
those on foot or bike. Deer stalking
sometimes takes place on the estate.

Start the walk by heading up the glen on
the track. Beinn Talaidh – which is in
distant view directly ahead – is named
after cattle and you may soon be
encountering small herds as they can
congregate around the track. After passing
the whitewashed cottage at Kilbeg go
through another gate and leave behind the
forestry plantations to enter the open glen.
The track nears the river, with more spruce
trees, and crosses a wooden bridge over a
tributary. When the track forks keep right
to stay on the same side of the river.
Further on the track fords another

tributary burn to reach a striking memorial, consisting of a propeller from a Dakota plane which was being delivered from Canada to Prestwick near Glasgow on 1 February 1945. Having stopped to refuel in Reykjavik the plane was flying too low – possibly because of ice on the wings. The aircraft smashed into Beinn Talaidh near the summit before sliding down the snowy mountainside, ending up in a deep gully. Out of the eight crew members on board, three died in the crash but one of the survivors managed to escape the wreckage and call for help from a shepherd's cottage in the glen. Further details, including some remains of the wreckage, can be seen in Tobermory Museum.

Take the right-hand fork at the memorial and follow the track to the bothy at Tomsleibhe. Maintained as an open shelter for walkers by the Mountain Bothies Association it is a good place for a rest and a browse of the bothy book to see who has stayed and what they got up to recently; please help keep the place clean and free from litter. Beyond, the track becomes indistinct and boggy, petering out completely after crossing a burn. From here head south to reach a gate in the fence, after which the route starts to climb up the very steep nose of the mountain.

The gradient eases slightly at around 500m, with good views over towards Loch Ba to the right; Ben More dominates the surrounding peaks. The final pull over stony ground leads up onto the grassy summit plateau. A trig point and a large cairn mark the top, with wonderful views down to Loch Spelve and the A849 snaking below to the south. Return by the same outward route.

◂ Looking towards Ben More from the slopes of Beinn Talaidh

Coast to coast

Distance 4.25km **Time** 2 hours one way
Terrain track, then paths, very boggy in
places **Map** OS Explorer 374
Access Craignure to Tobermory bus
detours from Salen to the road junction at
Gruline on the B8035, 1km from start

Crossing Mull from coast to coast on foot
sounds like a major challenge – but this
route crosses the narrow neck from Loch
na Keal to the Sound of Mull, making for a
mini-adventure. After a break for
refreshment at Salen there may be time to
reverse the route and walk back if
transport hasn't been arranged.

On the B8073 just west of Killiechronan
there is a small parking area opposite a
short row of houses. Start by walking
along the road towards Gruline and Salen
(turn right as you face the cottages from

the car park) and then soon turn left up a
track beside the large boulder inscribed
'Killiechronan'. Take the middle track of
three here to climb uphill, before turning
right at a fork. Pass through a gate into
woodland, eventually passing a whitewashed cottage with a collection of
wooden sculptures and an impressively-
proportioned walled garden.

Looking back, the peak of Ben More rises
grandly above Loch na Keal. The track
continues to climb; at a fork just before the
forestry plantation branch right to head
through a gate into the trees. Birches and
flowering rhododendrons line the route
which lacks the oppressiveness of many
plantation walks. The track narrows to a
path, eventually bearing left and heading
through a short gated section with a fence
on either side. After this the path

◀ Climbing away from Killiechronan

deteriorates to somewhere between slightly soggy underfoot and a complete quagmire depending on recent rainfall. The trees thin as the route heads up onto the open moorland; cross a burn and continue climbing gently. A faint path coming down from Cnoc na Sroine to the left is marked by a tiny cairn; ignore this and continue ahead. Short detours may help avoid the boggiest sections as the route passes through the native woodland fragments at Doire nam Pioghaid.

Conditions underfoot eventually improve, and soon Salen comes into view before the mature wood of Airigh Mhic Dhom nuill is reached. Descend on the main path through this fine mixture of birches and mighty oaks. After weaving its way down through the trees the path emerges at a large old church, now converted into a private home. At the main road turn right to head into Salen which has a hotel, coffee shop and well-stocked general store.

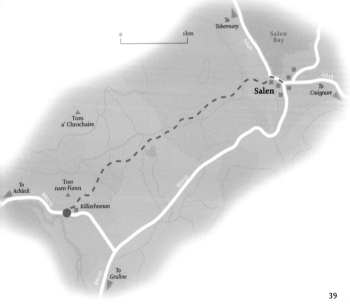

Loch Ba

Distance 4.75km **Time** 2 hours 30
Terrain good track, dry underfoot
Map OS Explorer 375 **Access** nearest bus
stop is at Gruline junction (B8035 &
B8073), 2km from start

The heart of Mull is wild and
mountainous, but this walk leads in
towards this unforgiving landscape
without any obstacles greater than a cattle
grid. The route heads along the shore of
Loch Ba before returning the same way –
giving a chance of eagle and deer
sightings amongst the livestock that
graze here.

Knock is a tiny settlement at a sharp
right-angled bend on the B8035. There is
space to park here on the track leading to
River Lodge. The walk begins along the
other track, passing a Benmore Estate sign
and double gates. This stony track heads
southeast towards Loch Ba.

As the track nears the water's edge a
driveway leads off to a lodge house;
continue ahead over a cattle grid to reach
the shore. The slopes of Beinn a'Ghraig
loom up on the right. As well as being
popular with ramblers and fishermen, this
track to Loch Ba is the start of a couple of
traditional routes over the mountains.

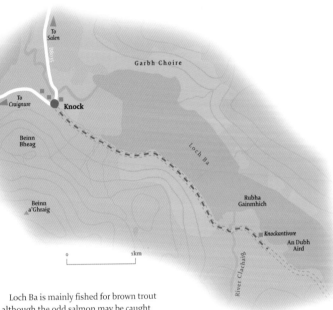

Loch Ba is mainly fished for brown trout although the odd salmon may be caught by the fly fishermen you might see out on the loch on the wooden boats of the estate. As the track rounds the corner and continues along the lochside, it passes a fish farm. Fishermen trying their luck on the water are provided competition by sea eagles whose flash of white on their tail feathers helps distinguish them from the golden eagles which are also resident on Mull.

Keep left at a fork in the track – the right-hand route leads up Glen Clachaig. Cross the River Clachaig on the bridge and keep an eye out for deer, although they are usually outnumbered by grazing cattle. Continue along the track until you reach the restored fishing bothy at Knockantivore and the promontories beyond, a good spot for a break and the turning point for the walk. The return is by the same easy outward track.

◀ Benmore Lodge and Loch Ba

Ben More

Distance 9.25km **Time** 6 hours (there and back) **Terrain** moorland and mountain path; hillwalking gear and navigation skills needed **Map** OS Explorer 375 **Access** no public transport to start

Mull's only Munro makes a popular and challenging day out. The usual route of ascent begins from sea level making for a long though steady climb; on a clear day the reward is a spectacular vista of mountain, land and sea. Deer stalking takes place on certain days from August until 20th October (not on Sundays) – between these dates the Benmore Estate should be contacted in advance for advice.

There is a large, informal grass parking area at Dhiseig on the seaward side of the A8035 just east of a bridge. Although keen and experienced hill walkers may prefer the challenge of approaching Ben More via the A'Chioch ridge scramble, the more straightforward route described here is much more popular, being shorter and suitable for those who are terrified rather than inspired by phrases such as 'airy scramble' or 'loose scree'.

Follow the track (SP Ben More) opposite the parking area, passing the entrance to the house at Dhiseig and spurred on by a sign that simply reads 'Up'. Pass through a gate and bear right alongside the Abhainn

Dhiseig which cascades downhill in a small gorge. Bear left by a fence for a short distance to reach a gate. Beyond this you are faced with a choice; two routes have been created by endless boots which rejoin further up; the left fork which continues following the Abhainn is more attractive and drier underfoot.

Ben More rears impressively ahead. Aim straight towards the peak, crossing a side burn on a worn route; ignore the path branching off left towards to An Gearna. The path becomes clearer and passes piles of stones - the remains of high sheilings. Cross the Abhainn Dhiseig at an easy spot and continue uphill on the far side, passing a series of waterfalls. The path keeps close to the burn at first before bearing right and becoming increasingly eroded. Higher up the route follows a better defined ridge and is marked by a number of small cairns; zigzags ease the going up the now steep and stony ground.

On the final stretch there are fabulous views back down over Loch na Keal and the islands, whilst ahead the dramatic A'Chioch ridge is revealed. Keep to the highest ground along the summit ridge heading southeast to finally arrive at the trig point, 966 metres above the sea. A large shelter of rocks helps keep the wind off, making a perfect spot in fine weather to enjoy your sandwiches whilst watching any scramblers emerging from the A'Chioch route. Unless you have the time and experience to tackle A'Chioch safely (in which case it is perhaps better done as an ascent route), the best return is to retrace your steps.

◀ Looking northwest from the summit of Ben More

43

Mackinnon's Cave

Distance 3.5km **Time** 2 hours
Terrain the final approach to the cave
crosses awkward, slippery boulders and is
tidal; it is essential to check tide times
before setting out **Map** OS Explorer 375
Access no public transport to start; the
parking area is near Balmeanach

Visited by Johnson and Boswell and once
considered a 'must see' by those
undertaking a Grand Tour, locating and
exploring Mackinnon's Cave – said to be
the longest sea cave in the Hebrides – still
provides a memorable experience. Don't
forget your torch!

To reach the start of the walk, follow the
surfaced track which leaves the B8035 just
west of Gribun; after some houses there is
a signed parking area on the right. It is
only possible to visit the cave when the
tide is at least halfway out. For this reason

check the tide times and attempt the tidal
section whilst the tide is still going out to
avoid the risk of being stranded – large
though the cave is, waiting for the tide to
recede is not recommended. Tide times
can be checked at Tobermory Visitor
Information Centre or online at
easytide.co.uk. The first part of the walk
passes through croftland, so dogs need
to be kept under tight control because of
the livestock.

Begin by following the lane to the farm,
keeping left at a fork and going through a
gate to take a rough track to the left of a
fence. When the corner of the fence is
reached turn right to keep the fence on
your right. This part can be very wet
underfoot, but the going soon improves as
a track is joined. Keep near the fence.
Ahead there are views out to the islands of
Staffa, Ulva, Inch Kenneth and the distant
but distinctive Dutchman's Cap as well as
numerous smaller islets. Pass through an
iron gate on the right and head down a

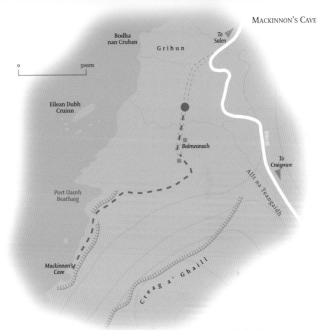

grassy dip before bearing left.

The view west is impressive, with dramatic cliffs and a high waterfall. The path heads down a rocky ramp to reach the shore. Continue across the bay until just beyond a low section of cliff; rather than being tempted to keep scrambling over the massive boulders towards the waterfall, look out for a grassy area to the left. From here a path keeps just above the rocks and boulders before descending to the foot of the falls.

Take care on the slippery boulders on the next tidal section. Work your way around or over the boulders to reach an inlet just beyond the waterfall. The yawning cave

entrance is now revealed. The cave soon twists and becomes so dark that you cannot even see your hand in front of your face; a torch is needed to negotiate the floor of sand and rocks. Johnson and Boswell visited by boat while on route to Staffa in 1773; they managed to explore for 150 metres (which they measured out with a walking stick) before returning when their candle burnt out. Boswell recorded that local tradition tells of a piper, his dog and twelve men that once entered the cave – only the dog re-emerged, terrified and almost hairless. So do take care. Should you make it out, the only possible route back is to retrace your steps.

◀ Looking along the cliffs

The Burg and the Fossil Tree

Distance 18.75km **Time** 5 to 7 hours
Terrain good but increasingly exposed
path and a rusty ladder before the final
rough shore section; check tide times
Map OS Explorer 375 **Access** no public
transport to start

**Stunning coastal scenery at the remote
western tip of the Ardmeanach Peninsula
as well as a visit to the famous fossilised
tree are the rewards, but this tough walk
is not to be undertaken lightly. The
ladder down to the shore in particular is
very exposed and not for the faint-hearted.**

The start is near Tiroran, reached by
turning off the B8035 towards the Burg.
After a gate the road deteriorates into a
rough track: continue driving for three
quarters of a kilometre until a parking area
is reached. Start the walk by following the
track, forking right at a branch which
passes above a beautifully-situated
cottage. After the hut at Dun Scobuill the

route climbs more steeply by a burn to
reach a couple of transmitter masts and
four cairns, traditionally used as a coffin
rest en route to the burial grounds.

For the next 2km the track crosses
wooded and open land before dropping
steeply in a number of zigzags to cross a
bridge over the Abhainn Beul-ath an
Tairbh. Soon another fork is reached –
go left – the right branch leads to Tavool
House, an activity centre. The now
smaller track winds through some fine
woodland to reach a gate and stile leading
to the Burg – one of the first estates to be
owned by the National Trust for Scotland.

Branch left again to pass the ruins of
pre-clearance settlements and a more
modern metal-clad cottage. The next
building used to be a compulsory stop for
anyone seeking out the fossil tree.
Chrissie MacGillivary lived at Burg Bothy
for 91 years and regaled visitors with
legendary tales over steaming cups of tea.

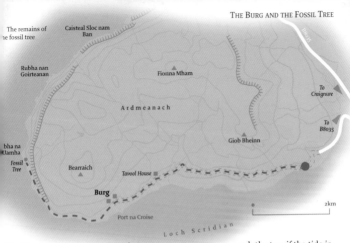

Continue across the grass towards Dun Bhuirg, the prominent mound on the left, site of an iron age fort. The more modern memorial is to Daisy Cheape, daughter of the local estate owner who died in a sailing accident in 1896. From here the walk gets much rougher underfoot.

Follow the grassy shoreline, which is pathless in places. Keep an eye out for the wild goats that roam the peninsula. The path soon becomes clearer as it begins to climb above the shore. All around is evidence of Mull's volcanic past with hexagonal basalt formations twisted into columns, curved fans and a distinctive wheel.

The drop to the shore is mostly precipitous, but it is possible to descend to the sea down a grassy slope immediately before the rocky rib that leads down to the wheel rather than continue to the ladder. This leaves a much longer rocky tidal section to negotiate but

means you can reach the tree if the tide is still heading out without taking the ladder. Otherwise the path winds through fallen boulders and runs along the edge of the cliff before a steep drop brings you to the top of the ladder. Getting a toe hold is the hardest move: a glance at the rotten remains of the previous ladder is no help to the nerves. Once at the bottom however, it is a short walk along the shore over a tumble of boulders to the Fossil Tree. The tidal section is best tackled on a receding tide so check tide times before setting out. Two impressive waterfalls cascade down the cliff before the the next bluff reveals a tall dark recess – the Fossil Tree. Thought to be 50 million years old it was formed as an imprint when the huge tree was engulfed by molten lava from Ben More. The bottom section once contained the original charcoal of the trunk but years of souvenir hunting means little now remains. The return is by the same outward route.

47

The landing point for the ferry from Oban, Craignure is the gateway to Mull for most visitors. The massive stone walls of Duart Castle make it an impressive sentinel when seen on the approach from the sea, backed by the high mountain ridge of Dun da Ghaoithe.

A fast highway speeds north along the Sound of Mull past Fishnish and the Lochaline ferry, but heading south the coastline becomes more complex and dramatic. The sea presses far inland at Loch Don, Loch Spelve and Loch Buie. The latter gives its name to a tiny hamlet with perhaps the finest setting on Mull, where rugged mountains form a backdrop to a fine beach as well as a great house, ruined castle, mausoleum and prehistoric stone circle. West from here the great coastal cliffs become ever more impressive, their secrets – caves, stacks and magnificent arches – revealed only to those prepared to explore on foot.

Cows on the beach below Ben Buie ▶

Craignure and southeastern Mull

Garmony Point and Fishnish

Distance 7km **Time** 3 hours
Terrain waymarked path, muddy in places
Map OS Explorer 375 **Access** bus to
Garmony Point from Tobermory or
Craignure

This walk skirts the attractive shoreline
from Garmony Point before looping
through the forestry at Fishnish,
overlooking the ferry to Lochaline.
A good walk for wildlife watchers with a
chance to spot otters and seals in the
water; the less fortunate will have to make
do with watching the progress of the ferry
across the Sound.

Start from the forestry car park at
Garmony Point, where picnic tables
overlook the Allt Achadh na Moine burn as
it flows out into the Sound of Mull which
separates the island from Morvern on the

mainland. The walk is waymarked in red
for the first stretch, following the signpost
for Fishnish and soon crossing a
footbridge. After a short section by the
road the route swings right over grassland
to reach the shore.

Continuing by the shore, boardwalks
ease the going over the wetter sections
before the path crosses a shingle bay. Mull
has one of the densest populations of
otters in the UK; though they can travel far
inland the best chance of spotting one of
these elusive creatures is off the shore.
Look out for the tell-tale V shape they
make as they swim and then once spotted,
keep a close eye as they are easy to lose.
With a quick flip of the tail they dive to
hunt for crabs, butterfish or eels, and can
spend up to 30 seconds underwater before
re-appearing just out of sight of your

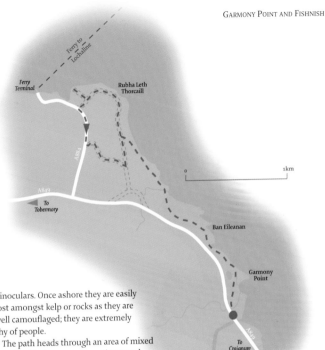

binoculars. Once ashore they are easily lost amongst kelp or rocks as they are well camouflaged; they are extremely shy of people.

The path heads through an area of mixed woodland before an open section reveals views across the water. Head through a gate into the forestry plantation to eventually emerge onto a track. Bear right to follow the track to reach the road. Just to the right is a car park and picnic area overlooking the Calmac Fishnish to Lochaline ferry. The ferry terminal itself has a snack bar which can be reached by following the road to the right. Queues for this popular (and cheaper!) alternative route to the mainland used to be legendary but in recent years the 36-car capacity *Loch Fyne* has plied the route

following its redundancy as one of the Skye ferries once the road bridge to Skye was built.

If not heading for a coffee turn left along the tarmac road for a short distance until a link path heads into the trees on the left. Follow this to a forest track, turning left and continuing a winding course through the woods to rejoin the outward route. Turn right to begin the walk back by the shore to Garmony Point.

◀ Across the Sound of Mull to Ardnamurchan

Scallastle forestry walk

Distance **4.75km** Time **1 hour 30**
Terrain **forest tracks and paths, steep and
stony in places** Map **OS Explorer 375**
Access **nearest bus stop is in Craignure,
1.5km from start**

The regenerating woodland on the
hillside south of Scallastle is explored on
this waymarked walk, which also offers an
attractive cascading burn and views across
the narrow waters that separate Mull from
the mainland.

The Scallastle Forestry Commission car
park is signed from the south side of the
A849 just north of Craignure. If
approaching from the north there is no
sign so take the next turning on the right

after the Isle of Mull Hotel. Begin by
continuing up the track from the parking
area with a view of Dun da Ghaoithe, the
only hill on Mull to attain Corbett status
(Scottish mountain over 2500ft), ahead.
As the track narrows the Sound of Mull
can be seen to the right.

The felled forestry here is part of a
scheme by the Forestry Commission to
reduce the number of conifers by felling
and leaving the slopes to regenerate with
native species. Some hardy birch pioneers
can be seen amongst the felled stumps.
Pass a picnic table and follow the route
alongside the remaining plantation before
crossing more open land.

Here you may stand a good chance of

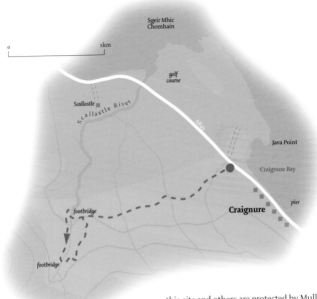

spotting a white tailed or sea eagle. The largest of the UK's birds of prey, its re-introduction has been a triumph for conservationists although their success is causing concern for crofters who blame them for taking lambs in some areas. Driven to extinction in the 19th century the birds were re-introduced from Norway and Mull is now home to about 11 breeding pairs. The RSPB hide at Loch Frisa operates escorted visits where you can see a nest site and CCTV images of the nesting birds. The birds are still under threat from egg thieves and illegal poisoning however, so

this site and others are protected by Mull Eaglewatch, a local volunteer group.

Ignore the steep path to the left (used on the return) and instead pass a small covered reservoir and head across the bridge over the Scallastle River. Bear left to head upstream beside the clear waters of the burn, with the mountains looming impressively ahead. When a bridge is reached cross it and ascend steeply on a stony track. Once the gradient levels off the route swings left and there are great views across the Sound of Mull. A fairly steep descent leads back down to the outward route. Turn right along this to retrace your steps to the start.

◀ Regenerating woodland at Scallastle

Torosay Castle from Craignure

Distance 6.75km **Time** 2 hours 30
Terrain good paths and tracks
Map OS Explorer 375 **Access** bus to
Craignure from Tobermory or Salen;
ferry from Oban

Follow the coastline from Craignure to
visit Torosay Castle and a beautiful bay
with views to Duart Castle, before
returning through Hedgehog Woods.

This circular walk can be combined with
a visit to Torosay Castle and Gardens to
make a grand day out. Start the walk by
following the A849 Fionnphort road south

out of Craignure passing the Craignure
Inn. Watch out for a track on the left next
to a picturesque lodge house; the track is
marked no admittance for vehicles. Take
this through a tree-lined avenue and keep
straight on when another track forks right.
There are great views across the water to
the mountains on the mainland and as the
track progresses Duart Castle can be
glimpsed through the trees across the bay.

The track passes above what was once
the station for the Mull Railway – now
unfortunately closed down – and soon the
track emerges just below the castle. To

visit the castle and the gardens just head to the right. It is worth taking the track down past the former station to head through the trees to a lovely spot with a cottage and jetty where there is a great view to Duart Castle.

To return, look for a small metal gate into a field opposite the parking area just south of the entrance to the castle. Take a diagonal line to the left up through the field to reach a second gate leading into the wood. The clear path climbs through the trees to emerge on a track. Turn left to follow this past an old water tank before it reverts to a narrow path. Just before a house is reached bear left onto the main road and turn right to take the pavement back down into Craignure.

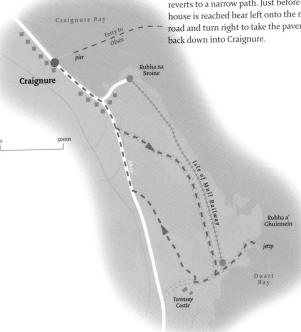

Catching crabs with Duart Castle in the background

Dun da Ghaoithe

Distance 15km Time 5 hours
Terrain Landrover track as far as the
masts, then pathless grassy ridges;
hillwalking gear and navigational skills
needed Map OS Explorer 375 Access no
public transport to start; you can also set
out from Craignure, avoiding much of the
main road by following the Torosay Castle
walk to near the start

The second highest mountain on Mull,
Dun da Ghaoithe is a prominent landmark
from the ferry to Craignure and
commands wonderful views over the
island and mainland coast.

There is only limited parking at the start
of this walk, reached by heading south
from Craignure and taking the next right
after the entrance to Torosay Castle. The
road climbs steeply and turns sharply right
before levelling off at a row of massive oak

trees. There is usually space to park
carefully here, but if not then you may
have to find room along the main road
and walk back. The walk starts by
following the road past Upper Achnacroish
to a gate and metal stile. Climb this and
keep following the track which climbs
gently. A backward glance reveals views to
Duart Castle with the Isle of Lismore and
Argyll behind. Behind Oban the two
summits of Ben Cruachan can be picked
out, whilst on a clear day Ben Nevis can be
seen further to the left. To the right are the
islands of Luing, Scarba and Jura.

After a zigzag, the track passes to the
right of the masts and buildings at Maol
nan Uan. Here the first view of Dun da
Ghaoithe is revealed – the right hand peak
of the two visible summits is the highest.
Branch right at a fork to avoid the masts
and climb a steep section of zigzags before

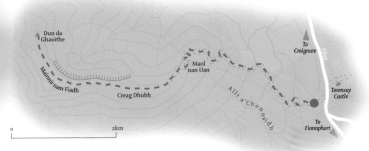

Dun da Ghaoithe

Mainnir nam Fiadh

Creag Dhubh

Maol nan Uan

Allt a'Chonnaidh

To Craignure

Toronsay Castle

To Fionnphort

0   2km

easier ground and a second cluster of masts is reached. Keep right of the fence here, leaving the track and other man-made features behind; from here there is no path. After a short sharp rise the broad ridge levels off to pass a couple of lochans.

After passing two rocky ribs bisecting the ridge, the route climbs more steeply and the ridge narrows towards the summit of Mainnir nam Fiadh. The top is marked by a massive cairn and a trig point, though our final objective lies another 1km away to the north west.

Continue along the ridge which broadens as it descends to the bealach between the two peaks. A stony slope leads up to the summit of Dun da Ghaoithe. This too is topped by an impressive cairn and the view is even better than that from Ben More, which is seen together with the A'Chioch ridge to the west. Unless intent on a long and much rougher traverse, the return is by the way you came.

Snow-capped peaks of the mainland from the summit of Dun da Ghaoithe ▾

57

Gualachaolish

Distance 8km **Time** 3 hours
Terrain track and path, very boggy in
places with a locked gate to climb; route
goes through grazing land – keep dogs
under tight control **Map** OS Explorer 375
Access nearest bus stop is at Lochdon,
2km from start

**An ancient (often waterlogged) path
leads to the abandoned settlement of
Gualachaolish in a stunning location
overlooking the entrance to Loch Spelve.**

Gualachaolish is one of many
uninhabited settlements dotted all over
Mull, evidence of the rapid depopulation
during the years of the clearances and
mass migration. The actual buildings at
Gualachaolish are better preserved than
most as they remained occupied by a
single crofter until the 1930s.

The unmarked start of this walk can be
hard to find so keep your eyes peeled.
From Lochdon take the A849 to the west,
continuing past the turning for Grass Point
on the left and a couple of forestry tracks
on the right. The start of the walk is the
small track entrance on the left just before
the road curves right. There is only room
for one carefully parked car here.

Head through the gate and follow the
grassy track. After wet weather the going
soon becomes marshy and is indistinct in
places. When the track forks keep right to
climb gently, crossing undulating ground
usually dotted with grazing cattle and
sheep. As the small hill of Carn Ban comes
into view carefully climb the gate and
follow the path across the open moorland.

Looking back there are good views of the
mountainous interior of Mull with Dun da
Gaoithe and Sgurr Dearg to the right (east)
and Beinn Talaidh further left. After

the house was home for the factor of the Possil estate which included Torosay and Duart. The house and steading would therefore have been larger than many crofters' properties from the same era. The main house was lived in by a crofter until the 1930s which is why the walls still stand to their present height. This is a lovely spot to while away time and perhaps watch for sea eagles circling above. For those who wish to explore further it is possible to detour to the old churchyard at Killean sited above a small sandy beach. There is no direct path and in high summer, when the bracken is at full throttle, finding the route can be a battle. However, aim west from the ruins at Gualachaolish, heading through a gap in the old stone wall downhill and slightly to the right, aiming WNW until the walled graveyard comes into view. Local folklore tells of a bone that was always buried with the latest coffin; by the time of the next burial the bone was always found to have returned to its resting spot on a ledge on one of the outer walls. From the graveyard you can follow a vague and boggy path alongside the burn to rejoin the return path at the ruins passed earlier; otherwise retrace your steps to Gualachaolish to return to the start along the same outward path.

crossing a small burn the path becomes clearer as it hugs the remains of an old stone wall. The waters of Loch Spelve can now be seen down to the right. Eventually the path descends to the left to reach the ruins of houses and enclosures at a burn. Follow the path on the far side and after a short distance the remains of the farmstead at Gualachaolish comes into view to the right, beside a lonely tree. A faint path leads up to the well-preserved and atmospheric ruins. Built in the 1800s,

◀ Farmstead ruins at Gualachaolish

Port nan Crullach

Distance 4.75km **Time** 1 hour
Terrain rough track, sometimes wet
Map OS Explorer 375 **Access** no public
transport to start

**Reaching secluded Croggan on the
southern shores of Loch Spelve can be an
adventure in itself. From this tiny
settlement the walk follows a lochside
track to reach the beautiful and very
peaceful beach at Port nan Crullach, a
perfect spot to let time drift slowly by.**

Travelling anywhere by road on Mull
takes time so it requires some
commitment to head out to Croggan,
situated in one of the furthest-flung
corners of the island, and accessed via a
lochside road that only just manages to be
single track; however, the landscapes are

stunning. Leave the A849 at Strathcoil at
the north end of Loch Spelve until
Kinlochspelve where you turn left at a
junction marked by an impressively robust
stone postbox.

Croggan itself comprises a small cluster
of houses and the rusting remains of a
large pier. There is limited parking just
before the phonebox; if parking on the
verge take care not to block any passing
places. From here the rough mountainous
heart of Mull is seen to great effect across
Loch Spelve, with dome-shaped Beinn
Talaidh prominent.

Start by heading to the end of the public
road and past the last house, continuing
on the track through mixed woodland.
Keep an eye out for a large mushroom-
shaped rock by the shore, a quirk of nature.

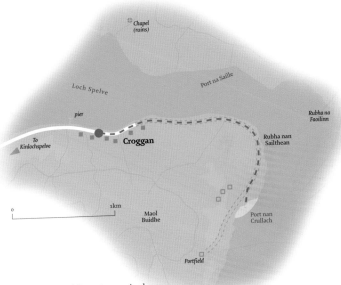

Chapel
(ruins)

Loch Spelve

Port na Saille

Rubha na
Faoilinn

pier

Croggan

Rubha nan
Sailthean

To
Kinlochspelve

0   1km

Maol
Buidhe

Port nan
Crullach

Portfield

At a fork, keep straight on to remain close to the shore, passing the ruins of a house before crossing a bridge over a burn.

Once past the mouth of Loch Spelve at Rubha nan Sailthean the views open up across the Firth of Lorn. The coastline of Argyll and its islands can be seen on a clear day with the Isle of Scarba just to the right. Another kilometre of track – boggy in places – leads to a sandy bay on the left. Port nan Crullach is little visited, a perfect crescent of fair sand providing a great picnic and wildlife-watching spot in almost any weather. Seals are fairly abundant, but porpoises and dolphins also pass this way and the very lucky, and patient, may be rewarded with an otter sighting (if not then Tobermory harbour is also a good bet

and you can try your luck while sampling the fish and chips!).

Once you have explored the beach, return by the same outward track. The remains of a settlement are close to where the track reaches the beach. Before the Highland Clearances and the mass migrations of the 18th and 19th centuries, Mull had a population of around 10,000. Today the permanent population of Mull is just 3,000, although visitors greatly swell the numbers during the summer. At less than 9 people per square mile it is sometimes hard to imagine the more populous coastline and glens of the island as they must have once been.

61

◄ Looking across Loch Spelve from the remains of a remote croft

Lochbuie explorer

Distance 8km **Time** 2 hours
Terrain minor road and rough track with
optional detour over boggy ground to
stone circle **Map** OS Explorer 375
Access no public transport to start

Remote Lochbuie occupies one of the
most beautiful locations on Mull. This
walk explores this magnificent setting,
taking in plenty of interest including
the church, the grand home of the clan chief, a
medieval castle, a sandy beach, a
mausoleum and a prehistoric stone circle.

At the far end of the public road, by the
shore at Lochbuie stands a stone pyramid-
shaped cairn, commemorating the
coronation of Edward VII in 1901 following
the long reign of Queen Victoria. There is
usually space to park nearby. Start the walk

by heading along the shore track towards
St Kilda's church (left as you face the sea).
Note the primitive sandstone cross built
into the wall of the porch – this was found
in the ground when building work on the
church began and is believed to be over
800 years old.

Keep following the track, passing
between two gateposts topped by orbs and
then over a bridge. Turn right through a
gate (SP footpath) and aim left alongside
the fence. Lochbuie House – seen over to
the left – was built in 1752 as the home of
the Chief of Clan MacLaine. It replaced the
medieval Moy Castle which is soon seen
ahead. This three-storey tower had all the
mod-cons expected of a castle in the 15th
century, including a garret, a first-floor
barrel-vaulted banqueting hall, a prison

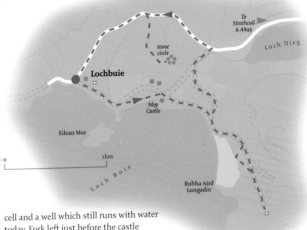

cell and a well which still runs with water today. Fork left just before the castle (SP Laggan Sands) to turn onto the drive of Lochbuie House. Turn right at a crossroads to reach a T-junction; you will return to this point later, but first turn right again to head out to Laggan Sands and the mausoleum. After rounding a bend the sands can be reached by descending to the right; otherwise continue along the track, branching right at the fork to reach the medieval chapel which was converted in 1862 into a mausoleum for the MacLaine family. Inside is an octagonal medieval font carved from Carsaig sandstone together with a number of gravestones and plaques including a prominent one in white marble commemorating the 20th Chief MacLaine who died in 1844.

Retrace the route back to the earlier T-junction and this time continue straight ahead, passing a number of cottages and heading through woodland before reaching the tarmac road. Turn left here,

passing a fine old schoolhouse. At the small parking area before the bridge turn left to follow the short detour to the stone circle. The white stones mark out a route across the boggy field but if you really don't want to risk wet feet it might be better to omit this part of the walk. Some of the boggiest bits have metal bridges – but others equally bad do not! Instead, keep to the right of a copse of trees and then turn left to follow a fence. The route soon becomes a track and leads to a gate – don't pass through this but instead head through a smaller gate along to the left. The stones are then reached over to the left. The well-preserved circle of 9 granite slabs is overlooked by the high flanks of Ben Buie. From the stones return to the road and turn left over the bridge, following the tarmac back to the start by the shore.

◀ Lochbuie House

Carsaig to Lochbuie

Distance **8.5km** Time **3 hours (one-way)**
Terrain **varied path, rocky in places, short
easy scramble; one section is impassable
at high tide** Map **OS Explorer 375**
Access **no public transport to start**

The linear walk from Carsaig to Lochbuie
is a real adventure with massive cliffs and
intriguing rock formations, a sea stack,
caves and waterfalls as well as lots of
wildlife. A return on foot by the same
route would make this into a full day.

Carsaig Pier is reached along the
beautiful but very narrow minor road
which is signed from Pennyghael. The
single track road has steep hills, sharp

bends and worryingly few passing spaces,
but when it arrives at Carsaig the setting is
idyllic. From the small parking area just
above the pier take the track opposite
heading east towards two holiday cottages.
At the first cottage take the path on the left
next to the gate. This delves in and out of
natural woodland, crossing a grassy area
which is wet underfoot. Soon the cliffs
loom high on the left and at very high
tides the route can become awash with
spray and waves.

The scenery becomes increasingly
spectacular with the high cliffs dotted with
caves and fluted into columns of basalt.
A waterfall forms a cascading curtain over

the entrance to one cave. The going gets easier as the raised beach between the cliffs and sea widens. The single sea stack is An Dunan, Gaelic for 'the fortress', a good description of this squat mass of columns. A section of well-built path hints at a time when this walk would have been a well-used thoroughfare linking two important settlements. At the drystone wall go through an iron gate and cross the burn. As the grass-covered raised beach narrows the path heads into the birch and oak woodland, broken up by stretches of rocky shoreline.

Soon a stony beach is reached and crossed – it is this section which is impassable at high tide. When a rib of rock bars the way a dangling rope marks the spot where you need to scramble up onto a ledge leading to the right. The route becomes easier again following a grassy section of raised beach and passing the walled entrance to the Uaimh nan Taillearan (cave of the tailors). Go through a gap in a drystone wall; the derelict farmhouse at Glenbyre comes into view across a pebble bay. Cross the burn near the sea and pass the front of the house to pick up a grassy track which leads to Lochbuie, passing through two gates and across the back of a sandy beach. Lochbuie has a beautiful and tranquil setting and can be explored more thoroughly on the walk on page 63.

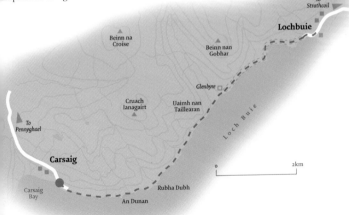

◀ The varied coastline of Loch Buie

Carsaig Arches

Distance **13.2km** Time **6 hours**
Terrain **rough and rocky coastal path;
optional dangerous exposed climb to
second arch** Map **OS Explorer 373**
Access **no public transport to start**

One of Mull's most celebrated walks, the
coastal trek to the impressive Carsaig
Arches is much tougher than many
expect. If you have plenty of time and are
well equipped this is a memorable outing
with superb cliff scenery and the possible
added bonus of encounters with wild
goats along the way.

The Carsaig Arches are rightly popular
but like much of Mull's rough coastline the

terrain leading to them is very rocky and
hard going; it should not be undertaken
lightly. If continuing to the second arch
extreme care is needed as the slippery path
is unprotected and dangerous – a wrong
footing could prove fatal. Most walkers will
happily omit this and return from the
gaping hole of the first arch.

The walk starts from Carsaig Pier,
reached along the single track signed road
from Pennyghael. This road can be
something of a trial for nervous drivers as
there are steep drops off the side of the
tarmac and few passing places. The pier is
likely to be reached with some relief but it
is a lovely spot, often with seals playing in

◄ The first of the arches

the water nearby. From the parking area head back up the road briefly, turning left along a track marked 'No Through Road'. This follows the shore and passes a caravan; when a junction is reached, bear left past a gate aiming for the beach. Continue round to a gate and then bear left onto the stony foreshore, fording a small burn to cross to the far side of the bay.

Pick up the path which leads to a kissing gate in the stone wall after which there is a short muddy section. Do not take the path seen rising steeply straight ahead – it is strictly for mountain goats and their kin. Instead follow the rocky shore, picking up the path again once past the landslip debris. The path sticks close to the shore – look out for birds and the odd seal bobbing curiously like a bottle in the water. Some sections of the path are eroded so care is needed. Look out for a striking pale cliff housing the wide gaping mouth of the Nun's Cave, a large shelter said to have been used by nuns outlawed from Iona by Columba who saw women (and cows!) as mischief making. If you can overcome the strong smell of goat, look out for the carved crosses on the left side as you peer towards the back of the cave; it is thought these might date from the 6th century.

Continue along the coast, passing a waterfall and with views out towards Jura and Islay. After a ruin at Malcolm's Point and a bouldery section, a slight climb brings you to the viewpoint for the first arch. A deep inlet separates this spot from the arch but it's a great place to soak up the atmosphere and watch the seabirds in the water below or nesting on the cliffs.

The second arch – which is smaller but more distinctive with a chimney-like stack on top – can only be reached by following a very narrow path up above the layer of basalt columns; this crosses the cliff above the first arch before descending steeply. A glance at this path makes its dangers obvious and it cannot be recommended. The most confident walkers with a strong head for heights may tackle it, but others should leave it for the goats! The return to Carsaig Pier is by the same outward route.

Often overlooked by day visitors hurrying to catch the ferry to Iona, the Ross of Mull is a low-lying but rugged peninsula with much to offer for walker and wildlife watcher. The walks here have great variety, from the impressive remains of the pink-granite quarry at Tormore, to the adventure of crossing the tidal sands to reach Erraid – inspiration for Robert Louis Stevenson's *Kidnapped*.

The main settlements of Bunessan and Fionnphort have between them a useful smattering of shops, places to eat and stay. The interior land is mainly rough grazing dotted with the ruins of deserted settlements and lonely crofts. The coastal cliffs are lower than those to the east, but shelter some beautiful sandy coves. With its extensive coastline and inland crofts, the Ross of Mull could easily keep you busy for a week or two's holiday.

The Ross of Mull

Shiaba and Scoor

Distance 6.25km **Time 2 hours**
Terrain rough track, some pathless
walking, boggy in places; track to start
very rough **Map** OS Explorer 373
Access no public transport to start

**Discover the ruins of Shiaba. Once home
to over 350 people, the inhabitants of this
thriving village were evicted from their
homes during the Highland Clearances.**

Reaching the parking area for the start of
this walk is a bit of an adventure in itself.
Take the minor road signed for Scoor to
the east of Bunessan off the A849. This
passes along the north side of the
surprisingly large expanse of fresh water,
Loch Assapol, before the road deteriorates
into a bumpy track. Pass some caravans
and a house at Tir Chonnuil, climbing
slightly to reach the small parking area
where the track forks. Over to the right the

remains of the medieval chapel and
cemetery can be seen.

This walk takes the left-hand track
marked with a red arrow, soon leading to a
cluster of houses at Scoor. Keep to the left
to pass the first cottage and then the front
of Scoor House. The track goes through a
gate before swinging right to head uphill.
Go through another gate into a field, after
which the track fades out. Pass just to the
right of the sheep fank to reach another
gate and stile giving access to a clearer
section of track. At the fork it doesn't matter
which branch you choose as the track soon
peters out once more; aim just left of the
grassy knoll. The ground falls away to the
flat moor beyond this; head left, keeping
the drop on your right, aiming towards an
obvious break in the forestry ahead.

Traces of a path soon dip down to the
right and meet a slightly clearer track. Turn
right along this to reach Shiaba. The ruins
of the settlement are now protected as a
Scheduled Ancient Monument due to the
almost unique preservation of its runrig

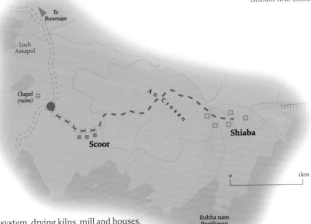

field system, drying kilns, mill and houses.

The house with the gable walls still standing is said to have belonged to the local schoolmaster and there would have been enough families here to sustain a sizeable school. The village was also home to the Gaelic poet Mary MacLucas.

Several factors combined to cause Shiaba's near abandonment. Firstly, the kelp market collapsed when protectionist taxes designed to stop the market being flooded by cheaper imports from Spain were abandoned. Landowners looked for a way to replace the lost income from kelp, and the Industrial Revolution was fuelling the market for wool. Many landowners on Mull, including the Duke of Argyll at Shiaba, began serving eviction notices on their tenants as a way to make room for sheep. Some tenants initially thought the eviction notice was an attempt to get them to pay more rent; however, when it became clear that their removal was being demanded they

petitioned the Duke. Included in the petition was this part of a letter from the oldest tenant of Shiaba:

'I am now verging on one hundred years of age,' Neil MacDonald wrote in 1847. 'It would be a great hardship and quite unprecedented to remove a man of my age who, is as natural to suppose, is drawing close to the house appointed for all living.'

However, the pleas of the villagers were ignored and they were dispersed to less fertile parts of Mull, with many choosing to emigrate to the New World. Shiaba was one of the first of the Mull Clearances and became a catalyst for further evictions in the following five years; a poorhouse was eventually built in Tobermory to cope with the impoverished homeless. A shepherd and family were installed here until the 1930s when Shiaba was finally abandoned completely to the sheep.

◀ Schoolmaster's house

Kilvickeon Beach

Distance 2.5km **Time** 1 hour
Terrain easy track **Map** OS Explorer 373
Access no public transport; 3km on very
rough road to starting point

**Pack a picnic for this short walk to a
stunning sandy beach, complete with a
tiny tidal island.**

This walks starts from the same spot as
the Shiaba route (p70) – a test for both
map-reading skills and your car's
suspension. Turn onto the minor road
signed for Scoor just east of Bunessan on
the A849. When the public road ends the
continuing track is very rough and
potholed for the remaining 3km. The track
passes a house and a couple of caravans
before it reaches a parking area. Here an

arrow marker points to the start of the
walk on a track directly opposite the
parking area.

After a short distance it is worth making
a detour to the right to visit the
atmospheric Kilvickeon Chapel and
graveyard; the loch makes a picturesque
backdrop. The chapel is medieval, probably
dating from the late 12th century and
would originally have been thatched. Near
the entrance on the north outer wall is a
very worn carved stone, probably a 'sheela-
na-gig'; a female figure displaying her
private parts. There are many of these
figures around Britain and especially

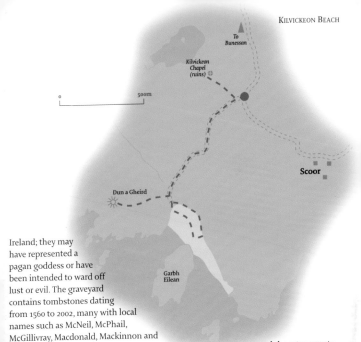

To
Bunessan

Kilvickeon
Chapel
(ruins) ✛

0   500m

Dun a Gheird ☼

Scoor

Garbh
Eilean

Ireland; they may
have represented a
pagan goddess or have
been intended to ward off
lust or evil. The graveyard
contains tombstones dating
from 1560 to 2002, many with local
names such as McNeil, McPhail,
McGillivray, Macdonald, Mackinnon and
MacLean. The chapel itself was replaced by
a newer church erected at Bunessan in 1804
and some of the stones from this chapel
were used in its construction.

From the chapel return to the track and
bear right, soon passing through a gate
and gently climbing. Once over the brow of
the hill descend the grassy track towards a
gate. Pass through this, bearing left to aim
directly for the beach.

The beach is a perfect arc of white sand
divided by the tidal island of Garbh Eilean.
It's a great place for families with plenty of
rockpools to explore, wildlife to watch and
good sand for castle building. If feeling

energetic you can extend the return route
by climbing above the beach for a
panoramic view from the site of an ancient
fort. To climb Dun a Gheird, head back up
the grassy slope from the beach and
instead of going through the gate continue
up the hill. At the top of the slope, which
can be very wet underfoot, bear left aiming
for the highest ground where the remains
of the outer wall of the rectangular fort
can be made out. The site is well chosen
as you can see for miles along the coast on
a clear day. From here return to the gate
and then retrace the outward route back
along the track.

◀ Rugged coastline from the beach

Aoineadh Mor and the Fossil Leaves

Distance **3km** Time **1 hour 30**
Terrain **rough, pathless moor and coast,
wet underfoot in places** Map **OS Explorer
373** Access **nearest bus stop is at
Bunessan, 2.5km from start**

**Explore Mull's wild coastline on this short
but tough walk to look for the remains of
fossilised leaves which put this spot on
the geologists' map. Today the wildlife
and views across to the Ardmeanach
Peninsula are the main draw.**

To reach the start take the road signed
for Ardtun from the east end of Bunessan.
Follow the waterside road before
branching left at a fork. Just before the last
two houses there is very limited parking at
the bend in the road, just beyond a stream
at a farm gate. Take care not to block the
gate or road.
Begin by heading through the gate and

aiming straight ahead for the prominent
lump of Dunan Mor.

This rocky outcrop is topped by a cairn
and is a great viewpoint; the name means
'big fort' in Gaelic though nothing remains
of this today. From the high point continue
walking in the same direction across wetter
ground to eventually reach the top of a
wide grass and stone ramp which gives
access down to the bottom of the cliffs.
At the bottom, aim right along the broad
coastal strip, probably a raised beach
indicating the change in sea levels since
the ice age. A number of ruined buildings
show that this strip of farmland was once
home to a scattered settlement.

Mull's volcanic past can be seen in the
basalt columns that make up the cliffs –
Staffa, famed for its own columns, is only a
few miles across the sea. Eventually the
route ahead is barred by a deep, steep-

◀ Dramatic cliffs seen from the path

Rubha Breac

Dunan Mor

Achnahard

Loch na Lathaich

Eorabus

Ardtun

0   1km

Lower Ardtun

To Bunessan

sided inlet where the waves roar below. Avoid this impassable obstacle by turning towards the cliff, heading back slightly to pick up a steep path which threads diagonally to the right up the cliff. Although the path takes the easiest ground it is still a steep pull up to the clifftop. At the top, bear left and enjoy great views of the massive cliffs of Ardmeanach across the water.

A gully, floored with fallen rocks and grass, soon forces you inland. From the head of this gully, well back from the sea, follow a faint path down into it, soon reaching a lower section strewn with fallen rocks. Care is needed in the gully; the path becomes clearer as it reaches a flat area where the remains of fossilised leaf beds are still visible. To the untrained eye the narrow bands of dark fossilised leaf mould can be hard to pick out. Look for the darker lines between the grey rock. These were made from the leaves of trees growing here

in prehistoric times and which fell into a loch every year building up between layers of mud and sand to eventually become fossilised rock. The leaf beds were discovered by the Duke of Argyll in 1851, soon leading to a stream of amateur geologists visiting the site. In the resulting rush of visitors many of the leaf beds were scraped away, leaving deep grooves in the rocks. One leaf bed you can't miss is on the right-hand side as you look out to sea with the words 'Fossilised Tree' carved above it. The sharp-eyed may find fossils on the gully floor showing patterns of leaf veins from leaves growing here about 54 million years ago, around the same age as the famous Fossil Tree on the Ardmeanach Peninsula.

To return to the start climb back up the gully and follow a vague path running back along the top of the cliffs before aiming directly for Dunan Mor to retrace the outward route.

Camas Tuath

Distance 3.75km Time 1 hour
Terrain good path, mainly level
Map OS Explorer 373 Access no public
transport to start

A short walk to the attractive bay and old quarryworkers' cottages at Camas Tuath, now used as an activity centre by the Iona Community.

The start of this walk can be hard to find. It begins on a track located off the A949 Bunessan to Fionnphort road, on the right-hand side of the road if approaching from Bunessan, directly after the entrance to Ardfenaig Farm. There is limited parking and a shed and bin at the entrance, with a sign for 'Footpath to Camas'. Begin the walk by heading through the gate, following the track to quickly pick up a boardwalk on the left. The grazing land on either side is a popular haunt of hungry geese during migration; watch out also for lapwings and curlews during the summer months.

As the track narrows to a path it crosses open moorland, passing through a gate before swinging right. Keep on the main path, ignoring any side turnings. The rocky outcrop ahead serves as the base for the turbine that brings power to the Camas Centre. Located in the old quarrymen's cottages down at the bay it is run as an outdoor activity centre by the Iona Community and youth groups can often be seen kayaking, building or falling out of rafts, or abseiling on the nearby crags.

Rubh a'
Chlaidheimh

Camas Tuath

Carraig
Ghilliondrais

Beinn nan Gabhar

Sithean
Riabhach

Cnoc
Deuchainneach

An t-Ard

Ardfenaig

Loch Gaol

To
Fionnphort

Abhainn

To
Craignure

0   1km

     As the path heads downhill alongside a well-constructed wall, ignore the signed path for Market Bay and continue ahead to reach the cottages. Please respect the privacy of the Camas Centre and follow the path to the right when you reach the bay. The quarry and jetty can be seen across the water. Although not as finely grained as the pink granite at Tormore, the hardwearing rock was still sought after and was used in the construction of the massive Skerryvore and Ardnamurchan lighthouses in the 1840s. The stone would have been transported from the quarry to the jetty by a tramway.

     The return is the same way, though you could decide to make a detour to visit the sandy beach at Market Bay. The path is signed on the right, is rougher going and takes about 20 minutes. The soft sand is a rarity on Mull and these days is a popular stopping point for sea kayakers. In the past cattle were swum ashore here from Tiree at the start of their epic journey to markets on the mainland. At low tide a scramble around the rocks leads to another area of fine sand. From Market Bay retrace your steps to the main path and head back up this to the start.

◀ Crossing the moor to the hidden bay

Tormore Pier and Quarry

Distance **2.5km** Time **1 hour 30**
Terrain **rough path, sometimes boggy,
steps and stony track** Map **OS Explorer 373**
Access **bus (496) to Fionnphort from
Craignure**

**Cross a coastal headland to reach the
hidden anchorage and sandy beach at
Tormore on this short but rough
exploration from Fionnphort. The route
then climbs through the old granite
quarry which was the source of the rock
for Iona Abbey.**

There is a large free car park near the
Columba Centre, signed from the main
road in Fionnphort. From here begin the
walk by returning to the main street and
turning briefly left towards the ferry. Just
before the shop cross the road to take the
minor road opposite, and then head left

before the trees to head out onto the
beach. A large erratic boulder, dramatically
cleft in two, sits in the middle of the bay.
Local folklore states that it split after being
thrown in anger by the giant Fingal.

Head across the back of the beach to pick
up an indistinct path leading around the
coastline. As the path winds between rocky
hummocks it becomes more obvious,
staying some distance from the coast itself,
but is wet underfoot in places. On a clear
day you get a great view of Iona Abbey
across the water. Keep an eye out for a few
blue waymarkers which are easy to miss,
but as long as you keep working your way
around the coastline you should soon
reach the slope down to the house and pier
at Tormore. To the left the sandy beach
makes an attractive place for a break; see if
you can spot Uamh na Marbh – 'the cave of

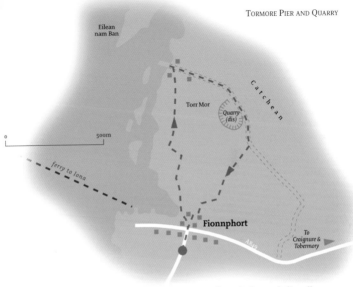

the dead' – supposedly used as a place to shelter coffins on their way to burial. To the right of the safe anchorage known as the Bull Hole is an island, Eilean nam Ban, to which St Columba is said to have banished women from Iona.

Nowadays Tormore is a peaceful spot, far removed from the days when the pier was used for the transport of the granite extracted from the nearby quarry. Follow the remains of the tramway uphill from the pier, passing a few houses. Continue through the dramatic entrance to the lower section of the quarry. Although now disused, the fortuitous combination of attractive and exceptionally hard-wearing rock and easy accessibility to the sea made pink granite from the Ross of Mull highly prized. As well as local projects such as the

abbey, Mull granite has ended up all over the world and can be found in three London bridges, the Albert Memorial in Liverpool and the docks in New York, as well as in buildings in Australia and New Zealand.

Take care in the quarry as there are steep drops and some rusting equipment left from when the quarry was last operational in the early 1990s. Climb the steps at the back to reach the upper level where there is an information board. Leave the quarry by the stony track, heading downhill. Just before a gate turn right onto a faint path which crosses grazing land, boggy in places. Keep straight on and the path eventually emerges at some houses. From here follow the road past the old graveyard and up to the main road at the start.

◀ The split boulder of Fionnphort beach

Traigh Gheal

Distance 9.5km **Time** 3 hours 30
Terrain path very boggy and overgrown
in places **Map** OS Explorer 373
Access no public transport to start; nearest
bus stop is at Fionnphort, 4km away

Traigh Gheal is a remote sandy beach,
reached only by sea or this tough walk
through the Tireragan Nature Reserve.
Since grazing by sheep and deer was
restricted on the reserve nature has taken
over and trees have begun to regenerate.
Whilst bursting with biodiversity, the
walk can feel like a jungle yomp at times
and is very wet underfoot.

The start is 4km south from Fionnphort.
Pass the farm at Fidden and continue until
the white house at Knockvologan; the
parking area is 100m further along on the
left. Walk along the road to the group of
agricultural sheds where there is an
information board about the nature

reserve at Tireragan. The reserve is
managed by the charity Highland Renewal
which has sought to restore the native
woodland. Go through the gate on the left
next to the board, passing between the
buildings. The track is grassy at first but
soon becomes stony. When it reaches a
gate, pass through to follow a path aiming
right across the heather moorland with a
drainage ditch on the right.

A footbridge and another gate and stile
lead to the entrance to Tireragan Nature
Reserve. With the assistance of public
funding trails were made and fencing
erected to restrict access to sheep and deer,
leaving the natural vegetation to thrive.
The path immediately forks; take the left-
hand path to climb onto Tor Fada which
has great views back over the beaches
towards the islands of Erraid and Iona with
its abbey visible on a clear day.

Continue along the ridge and after

heading slightly downhill another
path joins from the right which can be
used as an alternative route back. Ahead
cross an area of flat moor – usually wet
underfoot – and descend into a dip to
reach a stone waymarker. Keep straight
ahead here to cross a wooden footbridge
and bear left near the burn. At another
stone marker take the right fork – the left
branch is an optional detour to the ruins of
the settlement of Tir Fheargain on a rough
path. Unless taking the detour, keep on the
path as it heads southeast through dense
swathes of hazel and willow, passing the
remains of a second settlement, Breac-
achadh. The path keeps to the right side of
a shallow glen as it heads towards the sea;

the final section is often very boggy
and overgrown.

It is a relief to reach the superb beach at
Traigh Gheal, a stunning setting that
makes every squelch worthwhile. This is
a delightful spot to picnic, watch the
wildlife or just laze in the sun (or misty
rain). The return route is the same way,
with the option of turning left at the
junction below Tor Fada to pass the hill
on its southern side.

Erraid

Distance 6.5km **Time** 2 hours 30
Terrain tidal sands (check tides before
setting out), muddy paths, optional steep
climb to Cnoc Mor **Map** OS Explorer 373
Access no public transport to start

**The tidal island of Erraid was already a
magical place before Robert Louis
Stevenson added a dash of mystery by his
use of it as a location in _Kidnapped_. The
walk crosses the tidal sands to reach the
island before climbing to the highest
summit for views over Iona and
numerous other islands.**

As a tidal island Erraid is cut off at high
tide, with the locals relying on boats to
ferry themselves to Mull. This walk begins
with an enchanting walk across the sands
which separate the island from Mull. To
ensure a safe and enjoyable trip with no
mad dash against the incoming waters at
the end check the tide times and aim to
start out about an hour after high tide,
which should allow plenty of time for the

walk. To reach the start take the road past
the Columba Centre in Fionnphort,
passing the farm and campsite at Fidden.
Continue until a white house and then
look out for a small off-road parking area
100m further on the left. Begin from here
by walking along the road passing two
barns before going straight ahead through
a gate and onto a track. Follow this uphill
to pass Knockvologan Farm and eventually
down to the shore.

Bear right to head north for a short way
across springy coastal turf, following vague
vehicle tracks. When a dip is reached aim to
the left to reach the sands, hopefully newly
uncovered following the high tide and
rippled by the action of the sea. Once on
the sand bear right to head through a
magical sandy gap separating Erraid and
Mull. Vehicle tracks and hoof prints from
cows and sheep show that you are not
alone in making the most of the receding
tide to access the island.

At the far end of the sandy gap, bear left

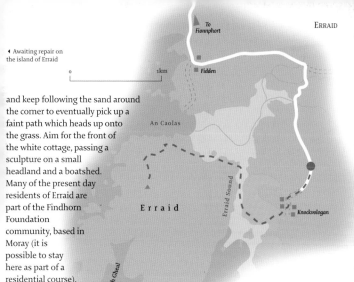

◀ Awaiting repair on
the island of Erraid

|0   1km|

and keep following the sand around the corner to eventually pick up a faint path which heads up onto the grass. Aim for the front of the white cottage, passing a sculpture on a small headland and a boatshed. Many of the present day residents of Erraid are part of the Findhorn Foundation community, based in Moray (it is possible to stay here as part of a residential course). Pick your way along the faint coastal path, crossing bridges over a couple of small burns before reaching a track which leads from the beach to the row of sturdy coastguard cottages. Climb the stile and follow the track as it passes the walled vegetable gardens and then bears left up through a gate, giving good views of the buildings at the jetty on the right. After the gate turn left and then – before the white gate leading to the cottages – turn right to head uphill on a rough path.

Go through the gate and continue as the path becomes clearer and passes a quarry where stone was provided for the cottages as well as Dubh Artach lighthouse 15 miles offshore. After passing a ruin turn left up a path which keeps to the right of a small gully. Ignore the stone steps on the right which are used on the return. Keep slogging uphill as it gets rougher and sometimes boggy underfoot. The climb is rewarded with spectacular views as the tiny cairn is reached marking the summit of Cnoc Mor, the highest point on Erraid.

Robert Louis Stevenson twice stayed on Erraid; his father David Stevenson was in charge of the construction of Dubh Artach (the Stevenson family built nearly all of Scotland's lighthouses). Retrace your steps from the summit, but branch left at a fork in the path to visit the communication tower built to relay signals to Dubh Artach and Skerryvore lighthouses. From here the stone steps lead back to the outward route which is then retraced to the start. Take care not to disturb the privacy of the residents of Erraid and stay on the main path.

Tobermory

Dervaig

Loch Frisa

Sound of Mull

Aros

Salen

Treshnish
Isles

Gometra

Ulva

Loch na Keal

Loch Ba

④ ③
⑤

Staffa

A part of this magical atmosphere must be due to the island's stunning natural beauty. Iona sits 1.6km from the west coast of Mull, with nothing to the west but the vast Atlantic. It has an array of beautiful coves, sandy beaches, green croftland and wild moorland, all set under an expansive sky. Small herds of hardy cattle often graze amongst the white sand and rockpools, seeking out the mineral-rich seaweed. These beaches are great places to watch for the steady procession of marine mammals that pass this way. The more remote coves provide havens for a mass of birdlife and the occasional otter.

Iona ①

②   ● **Fionnphort**
Bunessan
Loch Assapol

A849

Iona has been a place of pilgrimage for centuries, the monastery having been founded by Columba in 563. Despite the daily coach parties which fill each ferry for the short hop from Mull, the island still retains an aura of peace and tranquillity; those modern day pilgrims who come for a retreat with the Iona Community may still find the quiet here needed for spiritual reflection.

Ulva is an altogether different island, an undiscovered haven far from the usual tourist routes. A short hop across the Sound on the ferry makes possible a choice of excellent walks. The population of the island is just 16 but with a fine cafe, it makes the perfect destination for a relaxing day's walking.

Arriving by ferry to Iona

Iona and Ulva

Iona Abbey and the north end

Distance 7.5km **Time** 2 hours 30
Terrain minor road, grassy path to beach,
optional steep climb which can be wet
Map OS Explorer 373 **Access** bus to
Fionnphort; ferry to Iona

**Whilst the crowds on Iona follow in the
footsteps of pilgrims to the Abbey, this
walk continues beyond to explore the
northern tip of the island. The route
climbs the slopes of Dun I to reveal the
best view on the island before heading to
the northern beaches where cows munch
the seaweed on the white sands. A perfect
walk to complete a day on Iona.**

Originally dragged to Iona on the
insistence of Boswell, Samuel Johnson was
moved to write, 'That man is little to be
envied, whose patriotism would not gain
force upon the plain of Marathon, or
whose piety would not grow warmer
among the ruins on Iona'. Over 200 years
later Iona's many visitors are still drawn
here, whether motivated for spiritual,

personal or patriotic reasons, or simply by
a love for natural beauty.

Once off the ferry head up the street,
passing the shop on the left and following
the signs for the Abbey. On the right stand
the well-preserved ruins of the Iona
Nunnery. Turn right after this to pass the
primary school and dogleg to the right
along the road. Pass Maclean's Cross, an
elegantly carved high Celtic cross from the
fifteenth century; it is one of three on the
island, the other two being in the grounds
of the Abbey.

As the road climbs it passes the
impressively productive vegetable gardens
of the hotel, and then the Abbey is seen
over to the right. St Columba established
his mission here after landing from Ireland
in A.D. 563; there is a charge for admission

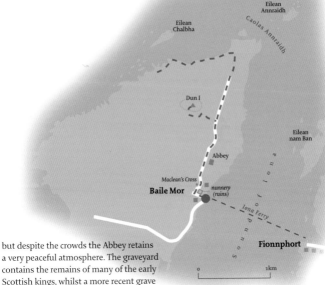

but despite the crowds the Abbey retains a very peaceful atmosphere. The graveyard contains the remains of many of the early Scottish kings, whilst a more recent grave is that of John Smith, the former leader of the Labour Party.

Bypassing the Abbey, the walk continues along the road, passing the Iona Community shop and then a few scattered houses and fertile grazing land. The hill of Dun I is prominent to the left and is well worth the exertion involved in reaching the top, though it can be omitted if short of time or energy. To climb the hill cross a stile just after a row of white cottages on the left. Head directly across the field towards the hill, soon climbing sharply. The summit is marked by a cairn and trig point and is a wonderful viewpoint.

Return to the road and continue heading north until it ends. Go through the pedestrian gate ahead onto a path between fences, then take the indistinct vehicle track straight ahead until after a grassy knoll on the left. Bear left to a bench and farm gate leading out onto the shore. Once on the sands you can head west across three beaches of perfect white sand divided by huge granite rocks.

The return walk is by the same route until the memorial stone opposite the Heritage Centre. Here turn down to the left to follow the narrow path, emerging on the main street only a few paces from the ferry jetty.

◀ Iona Abbey

Port na Curaich

Distance 8.5km **Time** 3 hours
Terrain minor road, moor and shore path,
sometimes boggy **Map** OS Explorer 373
Access bus to Fionnphort; ferry to Iona

**Leave the crowds behind to explore the
southern end of Iona, crossing some
stunning sandy beaches before reaching
the Harbour of the Coracle – the lonely
shore where St Columba first landed on
the island.**

The short ferry ride from Fionnphort is
as memorable for its fellow passengers as
for its beautiful setting. Catch an early or
late ferry and you may share with local
school children on their long weekly
commute to secondary school at

Tobermory – or a group bound for a
residential week with the ecumenical Iona
Community. As well as general sightseers
in great numbers, people from all over the
globe come to Iona on pilgrimage or to
take part in a retreat. Once on Iona most
passengers will head north towards the
Abbey, leaving this walk for connoisseurs.

From the jetty turn left, following the
road past Martyr's Bay bar and the tiny
Fire Station before reaching the war
memorial and a converted church. Remain
on the road as it swings inland and heads
west across the island. The road ends at a
gate giving access to the West End
Common Grazings which also double as
the local golf course. Keep straight ahead
on the track – giving way to any golfers –
and just before the beach turn left onto an

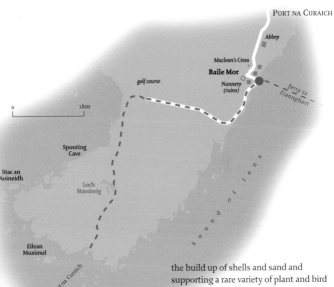

indistinct grassy track. There are great views over the sandy bay and unless the day is particularly calm look to the south along the coastline for distant views of plumes of sea water shooting into the air. These are caused by waves forcing water through a blow hole known as the Spouting Cave. The cave itself is not accessible though the water spouts can be seen from afar.

Where the track swings left towards a bungalow continue south to the far end of the golf course. Cross a bank of sand beside a fence onto the lush green ground of the machair – fertile land formed from

the build up of shells and sand and supporting a rare variety of plant and bird life. The track now climbs to reach Loch Staoineig. Leave the track here to follow a path to the left of the loch – the going is wet underfoot in places. The path crosses the moor before heading steeply down to a beautiful bay on the southern shore of the island. The shingle shoreline – divided in two by a rocky outcrop – is said to be the spot where St Columba landed on Iona. Having been banished from Ireland and forbidden to settle within sight of the Emerald Isle, he had first arrived at Dunaverty in Kintyre. Ireland could still just be seen on clear days, however, so he took to the sea again and this time reached Iona.

The southern part of Iona is very rough and it is best to retrace your steps back to the village.

◀ The Spouting Cave seen from the beach

Ulva shore and woodland

**Distance 6km Time 2 hours 30
Terrain waymarked rough path, boggy in
places Map OS Explorer 374 Access ferry to
Ulva (Monday to Friday; also Sunday in
summer); private taxi only to Ulva ferry
from Salen**

**The island of Ulva makes a perfect day trip
from Mull. This route explores the woods,
moors and coastline near the ferry jetty.**

The Ulva ferry operates on demand – just
slide the board to uncover the red signal.
The short crossing deposits you on the
eastern shore of the island at the
Boathouse which does a good trade in
home-made treats and hearty meals based
around local produce and seafood.

The name Ulva derives from the Norse
for Wolf Island, though it was inhabited
long before the Scandinavian settlers

came. The island's fascinating story is told
in Sheila's cottage – a heather-thatched
reconstruction of a traditional crofthouse;
to reach it head along the track and follow
the signpost.

To begin the walk proper, return to the
signpost and continue along the track,
almost immediately reaching a junction
with many signposts. Keep straight ahead
here and continue to a fork, then branch
left (SP Church). The peaceful creek on the
right would have been a hive of activity
during the kelp boom which reached Ulva
in the early 19th century. Kelp, produced by
processing seaweed, was much in demand
for its many uses including in the
manufacture of glass, soap and jelly. By 1837
records show that the population of Ulva
had grown to over 600. When the market
collapsed the population rapidly declined,
compounded by potato blight and then the

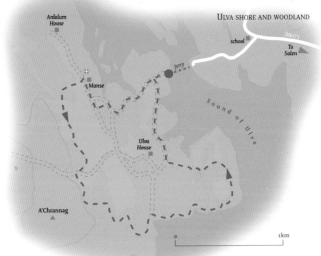

Highland Clearances. By 1851 three quarters of the population had been cleared by the owner Francis William Clark whose memorial will be seen later on the walk.

At yet another signed junction turn right and follow the good path which soon leads to Ulva church. Designed by Thomas Telford and built in 1828, the church accommodated 300 people. From the church follow the small path heading left up through the woods (SP Wood and Shore walk). After a steep climb the path emerges from the trees and bends left. At the next junction keep left (SP Wood and Shore walk) and head through more woodland and over a boardwalk before reaching a more open section. Keep to the left of the fence and in the next wooded area pass through the gate, continuing on down to a track. Go straight across this, keeping an eye out for the marker posts as the path is faint and muddy in places.

The route now heads over open moorland. The imposing Clark memorial can be seen on a hilltop over to the right. After a wooden boardwalk turn right at the fence and descend to a path junction. Go left here, following a fence downhill and passing through a gate to another junction. Continue straight ahead to the shore and bear right along the coast. There are great views across to Ben More and the Ardmeanach peninsula. This section crosses salt flats and can be wet underfoot; eventually a ladder stile over a stone wall brings you onto a path that heads left and then bears right up steps. The route now heads inland. A gate leads into the woods; turn sharp right and then left, passing ancient oaks. After a short open area go through another gate, passing a barn to reach a junction. A right turn leads back to the track above the Boathouse and jetty.

◀ Sheila MacFadyen's cottage

Ormaig and Kilvekewen

Distance 13km **Time** 4 hours (there and back) **Terrain** paths and tracks, rough in places and sometimes overgrown in summer **Map** OS Explorer 374 **Access** ferry to Ulva (Monday to Friday; also Sunday in summer); private taxi only to Ulva ferry from Salen

Explore the beautiful southern coastline of Ulva, visiting the atmospheric ruins of the former settlement at Ormaig and Kilvekewen church before returning in time for the ferry.

On a sparkling day, Ulva can really take your breath away. A small green and fertile isle separated from Mull by a narrow strait, it has impressive basalt cliffs and a rugged moorland interior. Always privately owned, in the early 1800s it was home to over 600 tenants living in 16 villages and

undertaking a number of trades mainly supporting the booming kelp industry where tonnes of seaweed were harvested and processed by hand. Within only a few years, however, the kelp industry collapsed, potato blight ruined the crops and the remaining starving population were cleared off the land to make way for sheep, triggering mass migrations with inhabitants of Ulva ending up in America, Canada and Australia as well as other parts of Scotland.

Today the only hustle and bustle is at the Boathouse where excellent teas and local seafood are served, well worth returning with time to spare before the return ferry. From here follow the track to the right and take the signed detour to visit the heather-thatched cottage. Once home to Sheila MacFadyen, it has been

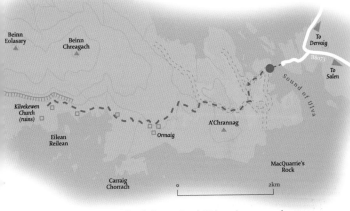

Beinn
Eolasary

Beinn
Chreagach

To
Dervaig

B8073

To
Salen

Sound of Ulva

Kilvekewen
Church
(ruins)

A'Chrannag

Eilean
Reilean

Ormaig

MacQuarrie's
Rock

Carraig
Chorrach

0   2km

restored as a small museum and includes Sheila's room with fire and cosy box bed.

Leave the cottage and follow the track uphill. Go straight ahead at a junction with many signs, then keep keep slightly left at a fork (signed Church). Turn left at the next junction, (SP Farm and South side) and continue ahead. At the farm buildings turn right following the sign for South Shore, heading uphill through trees past a water tank. After the trees keep straight on to follow the track over open moorland. At the next junction turn left and then continue ahead on the main track when the farm path leaves to the left. As it heads towards the coast there are wonderful views over the tiny islands dotted along the south coast of Ulva. A large cairn commemorating the village of Ormaig overlooks the site of the settlement and could be a good destination in itself if time is too short for the full walk. Ormaig is said to be the birthplace of General Lachlan MacQuarrie, the first Governor of New South Wales, whose mausoleum can be found at Gruline near Salen.

The ruins of houses can be seen on the left. The track passes a large tree and crosses a stream to head towards the shore. Keep an eye out for a signed path on the left just before the track bends towards the shore with a bothy visible ahead. Turn onto this path, which can be hard to spot if the summer bracken is in full growth. The path is the well-constructed old route between the villages, carefully contouring the side of the hill and passing more ruins. Just before a large rocky outcrop looms over the path the ruins of Kilvekewen church and the graveyard can be seen down on the left. It is possible to visit them by heading through the clearer bits of ground. The main path becomes much rougher after this point so the church makes a good spot to turn round and retrace your steps back to the Boathouse and ferry.

◀ The Boathouse cafe

Livingstone walk

Distance 7.5km **Time** 3 hours
Terrain rough waymarked path, muddy in
places **Map** OS Explorer 374 **Access** ferry to
Ulva (Monday to Friday; also Sunday in
summer); private taxi only to Ulva ferry
from Salen

**The grandparents of explorer David
Livingstone lived on a croft on the
southern shores of the island. This fine
walk has a suitably adventurous feel,
visiting the site of the croft as well as the
Livingstone cave and some impressive
and dramatic coastal scenery.**

Although David Livingstone never
visited Ulva, the old stories told by his
grandfather appear in his writings and
were a strong influence on his life. Like
many west coast inhabitants, David's
grandfather left the island in search of

work, ending up working in a cotton
factory on the Clyde along with his family.
They would have left behind a population
still in its hundreds though already in
rapid decline from its peak at the height of
the kelp boom, with Clearances and potato
famine still to come. Would they recognise
the island today, almost uninhabited save
for the cafe at the Boathouse and a few
farm workers?

From the jetty follow the track to the
right of the boathouse, detouring to the
right to visit the thatched Sheila's Cottage
which operates as an information hub for
the history of the island. Back on the main
track, continue west and go straight ahead
at the junction. Keep left at the next fork
(SP Church) and at the following junction
turn left to reach some farm buildings.
Turn right here to climb through the trees,

Eilean Garbh

To
Dervaig

B8073

To
Salen

ferry

Manse

Sound of Ulva

Ulva
House

A'Chrannag

Livingstone Cave

0   1km

passing a water tank and through a gate. Ignore the SP for 'the Farm and Shore walk', instead continuing ahead to emerge from the trees onto moorland. Turn left at the sign for Ormaig; after a sharp left bend fork left again onto a path following a stone wall to head steeply downhill through woodland. Follow the markers to the ruins of a cottage said to be that of Neil and Mary Livingstone. Bear left past another ruin, carefully keeping to the marker posts and climbing a bank to reach a sign. From here the Livingstone cave can be visited by a detour to the left. The shell midden (or ancient rubbish dump) here has revealed that humans occupied this spot 7000 years ago; the remains of lemmings and arctic fox were also discovered.

Continue on the path through a stone wall to reach the coastal cliffs with superb views of impressive basalt columns similar to those found on nearby Staffa; these were formed by the volcanic eruptions of Ben More over 60 million years ago. Pass through two areas of thick hazel, continuing ahead downhill at the signed junction. After being joined by another path bear slightly left before aiming left alongside a fence. After a gate turn inland (SP Ferry) along a rough track which passes through a farmyard, left through a gate and then bear right where a track curves towards Ulva House. Keep straight ahead at the next two junctions to pass between a pair of massive stone gateposts to rejoin the outward route back to the jetty and the Boathouse.

◂ Ruins of Livingstone's grandparents' home

Index